North American Color
"A Great Job"

[signature] '95

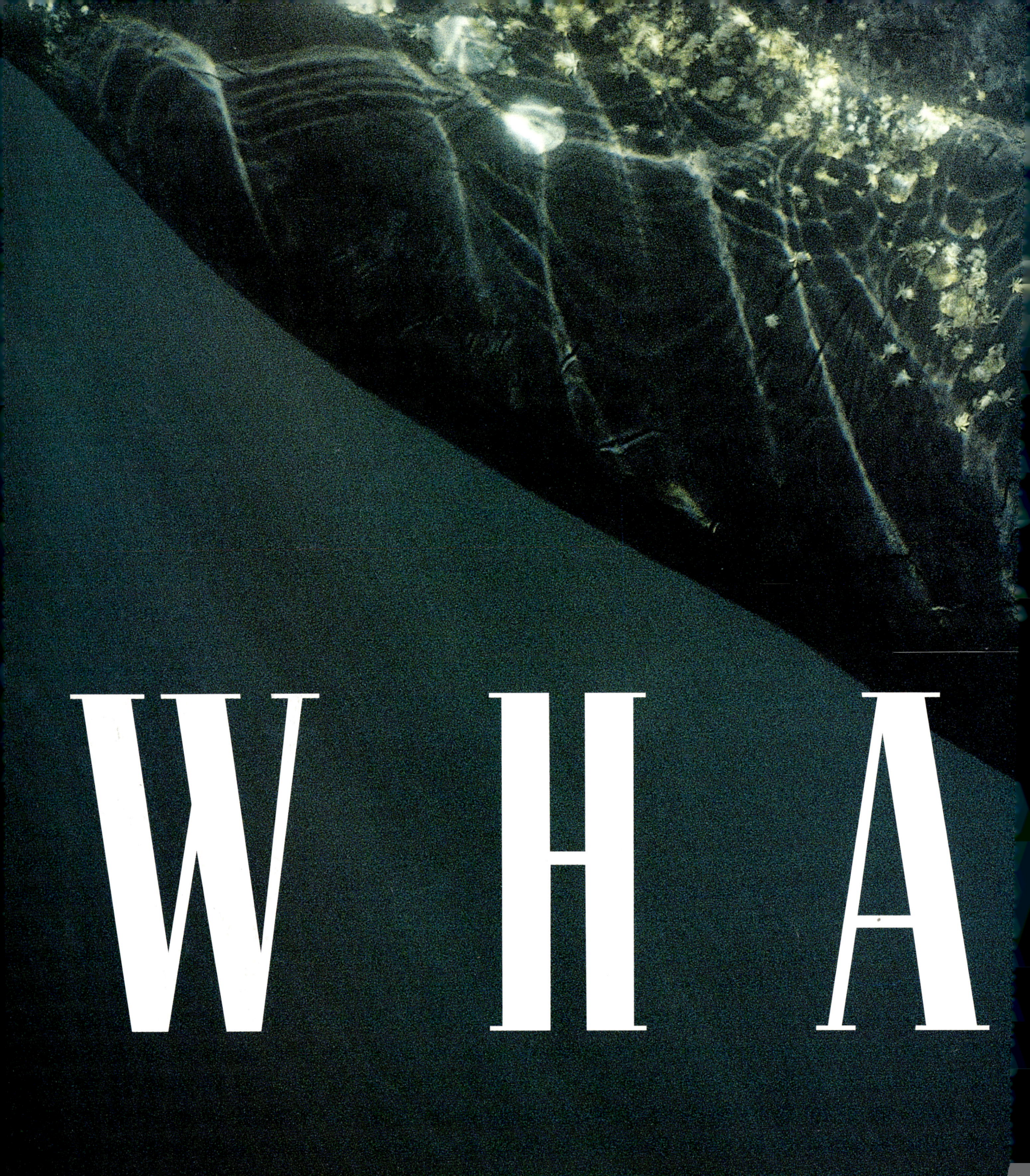

Prepared by the Book Division, National Geographic Society, Washington, D.C.

L E S

Dolphins and Porpoises

WHALES
Dolphins and Porpoises

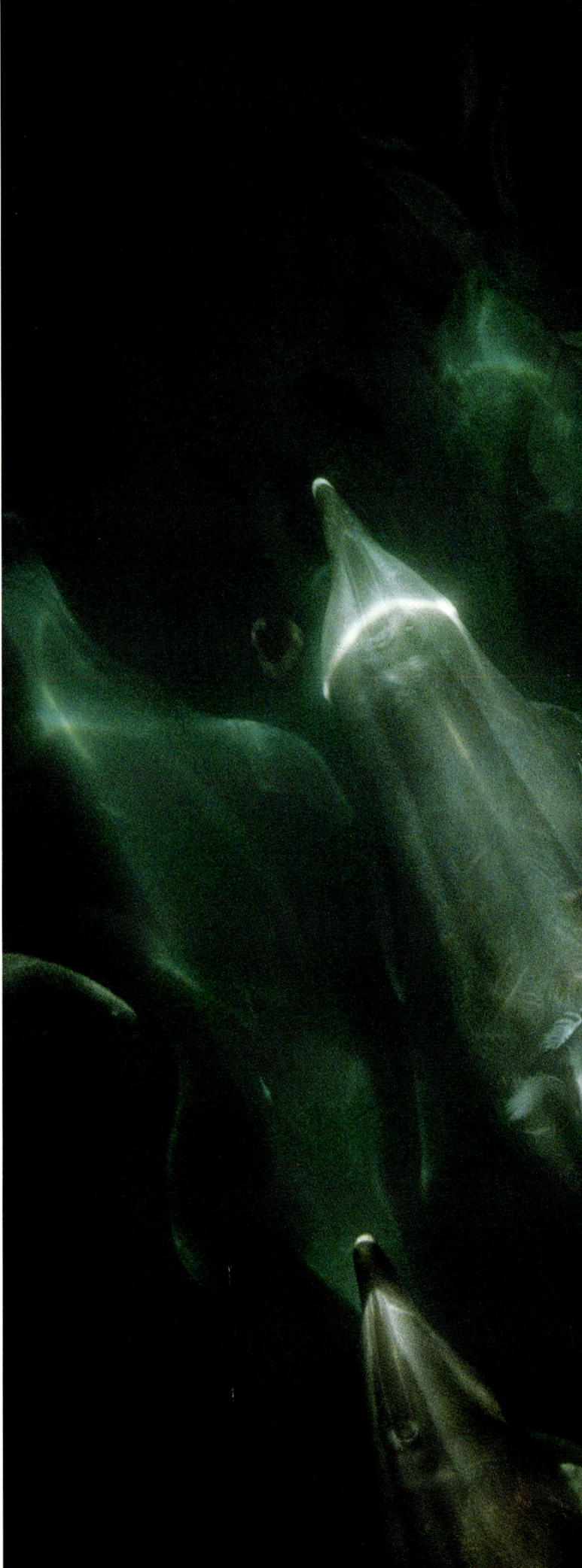

AUTHORS
James D. Darling
Charles "Flip" Nicklin
Kenneth S. Norris
Hal Whitehead
Bernd Würsig

CREATIVE CONSULTANT
Charles "Flip" Nicklin

ILLUSTRATOR
Pieter Arend Folkens

PUBLISHED BY
THE NATIONAL GEOGRAPHIC SOCIETY

Gilbert M. Grosvenor
President and Chairman of the Board

Michela A. English
Senior Vice President

PREPARED BY
THE BOOK DIVISION

William R. Gray
Vice President and Director

Charles Kogod
Assistant Director

Barbara A. Payne
Editorial Director

STAFF FOR THIS BOOK
Martha C. Christian
Managing Editor

Thomas B. Powell III
Illustrations Editor

Marianne R. Koszorus
Art Director

Tom Melham
Assistant Managing Editor

Victoria Anne Cooper
Senior Researcher

Ann Nottingham Kelsall
Joyce B. Marshall
Christy M. Nadalin
Researchers

Noel Grove
K. M. Kostyal
Picture Legend Writers

Margery G. Dunn
Contributing Editor

Lewis R. Bassford
Production Project Manager

Richard S. Wain
Production

Meredith C. Wilcox
Illustrations Assistant

Sandra F. Lotterman
Editorial Assistant

Elizabeth G. Jevons
Peggy J. Oxford
Staff Assistants

MANUFACTURING AND QUALITY MANAGEMENT

George V. White
Director

John T. Dunn
Associate Director

Vincent P. Ryan
Manager

Elisabeth MacRae-Bobynskyj, *Indexer*

PORTFOLIO:

PAGE 1:
Breaching humpback whale

PAGES 2–3:
Southern right whale

PAGES 4–5:
School of bottlenose dolphins

PAGES 6–7:
Southern right whale calf and mother

PAGES 8–9:
Juvenile sperm whale

PAGES 10–11:
Beluga whales

PAGES 12–13:
Gray whale

PAGES 14–15:
Bottlenose dolphins (captive)

PAGE 1: PIETER A. FOLKENS; PAGES 2-3: IAIN KERR / WHALE CONSERVATION INSTITUTE; PAGES 4-5: KEVIN SCHAFER & MARTHA HILL / GLOBAL PICTURES; PAGES 6-7: HOWARD HALL / HHP; PAGES 8-9: FLIP NICKLIN / MINDEN PICTURES; PAGES 10-11: JEFF FOOTT; PAGES 12-13: JOEL SARTORE; PAGES 14-15: FLIP NICKLIN / MINDEN PICTURES

Copyright © 1995
National Geographic Society.
All rights reserved.
Reproduction of the whole or any part of the contents without written permission is prohibited.

Library of Congress CIP data:
page 231

Foreword

17

THE PAST

Kenneth S. Norris

18

DEEP DIVERS

Hal Whitehead

46

SEINERS OF THE SEA

James D. Darling

82

REALM OF DOLPHINS

Bernd Würsig

138

THE FUTURE

Charles "Flip" Nicklin

202

Cetaceans: Life History Data 228
Index 230
Notes on the Authors, Acknowledgments,
Additional Reading, Whale-Watching Sites 232

WHALES
DOLPHINS AND PORPOISES

---------- FOREWORD ----------

For each of us, our first encounter with a whale leaves a lasting memory. For me, that experience came at age 16, near the Azores. Perched on the topgallant yard high up the foremast of the brigantine *Yankee,* I heard a shipmate shout—and I looked off our port bow. There, standing for an instant was a misty spout, then another, then the dark bulks of sperm whales.

I have never recovered. During the nearly half-century since that July day, whenever the chance has come, I have followed whales and the marine biologists who study them. Whether off the Galápagos or the Aleutians or the Hawaiian Islands, whales have always given me a sense of awe. I vividly recall my closest encounter in open water with these graceful giants of the sea: Out of the blue-green wilderness off Lahaina, Maui, a massive humpback whale glided toward me like a silent submarine. A huge brown eye above the enormous mouth seemed to follow my every move. Passing within touching distance, the whale gracefully lifted a gigantic flipper as if to avoid a collision. Later, I listened intently through a hydrophone, trying to make sense of its mysterious, enchanting songs.

I am astonished by the knowledge scholars have recently amassed. Of course, whale studies are a National Geographic Society tradition. Over the years, our Committee for Research and Exploration has awarded more than 60 grants for the study of cetaceans, and recent work has been breathtaking. Thanks to the U. S. Navy and its acoustic tracking network—opened to research in the early 1990s—we now know far more about whale migrations. DNA technology gives us insights into the genealogy of different species.

Yet our knowledge has come perilously late. Though we have dramatically curtailed the slaughter of whales, the future is clouded by an even deadlier danger: the pollution of our seas. Some populations pictured here may soon be extinct. Thus the unique nature of this book: As the 20th century moves into history, you hold in your hands a singular collection of photographs and a state-of-the-science summary of humanity's current, worldwide knowledge about whales.

Turning these pages, I recall the way I felt one night aboard a research vessel. Without warning, I heard a whale blow right beside the ship. In that magical moment, I sensed a closeness to that creature. I hope the following pages will bring you a similar feeling for these greatest of our fellow mammals.

Gilbert M. Grosvenor
President and Chairman of the Board
National Geographic Society

Twisted spire of a bull narwhal rears above the glassy surface of Milne Inlet off Canada's Baffin Island. Such tusks, usually limited to males, reach lengths of up to ten feet and serve both as weapons and as symbols in ritual displays.
FLIP NICKLIN

THE PAST

THE PAST

CHAPTER ONE

Kenneth S. Norris

MY GOAL WAS TO CAPTURE THE GRAY WHALE CALF OF A MOTHER-YOUNG PAIR, NOT THE FORMIDABLE MOTHER HERSELF. IT WAS FEBRUARY 5, 1975. I KNEW ABOUT THE TRAVAILS OF CHARLES M. SCAMMON, A WHALING CAPTAIN WHO HAD EXPERIENCED THE IRE OF ADULT GRAY FEMALES MORE THAN A HUNDRED YEARS BEFORE, WHEN HE VENTURED INTO THEIR CALVING WATERS IN THE LAGOONS OFF BAJA CALIFORNIA. NONETHELESS, I WAS BROUGHT UP SHORT WHEN THIS MOTHER, ANGERED THAT WE HAD HARNESSED HER CALF, TRIED TO SINK OUR 45-FOOT VESSEL. I WAS STANDING THIGH-DEEP ON A TIDAL FLAT WITH THE 14-FOOT-LONG YOUNG WHALE WHEN I SAW OUR CATCHER VESSEL RACING THROUGH THE MURKY CHANNELS OF THE LAGOON, THE IRATE MOTHER IN PURSUIT.

FACING PAGE: *Of 31 paintings of cetaceans in the January 1940* NATIONAL GEOGRAPHIC, *this one depicts a harpooned sperm whale.*
PRECEDING PAGES: *Bleached whale bones remain on an Antarctic beach once used for butchering the animals.*
ELSE BOSTELMANN (FACING PAGE); COLIN MONTEATH / HEDGEHOG HOUSE NZ (PRECEDING PAGES)

FURIOUS SEAS Tempest tossed, ships and whales ride out a storm in this late 16th-century painting by an artist known only by his initials, P.D.P., a member of the circle of Dutch artist Hendrik Cornelisz Vroom. The hunting of whales goes far back into human history. In the 12th and 13th centuries the Basques used small open boats and hand-held harpoons to hunt right whales in the Bay of Biscay. Right whales, they found, were easy to hunt because they are slow swimmers and they float when dead. As the local population of right whales decreased, the Basques and other European whalers began building bigger boats and venturing farther into the open seas. Dutch whalers rose to prominence in the early 17th century. In 1680 Holland alone had more than 250 whaling ships.

Swimming directly under the boat, she periodically swung her flukes up in an attempt to hit the craft racing above her. At flank speed, the frightened skipper steered his vessel over a shallow flat with only three or four feet of water beneath his keel. The whale did not follow, but it was only by our good luck that she had not sunk or severely damaged our ship. She had bent the ship's propeller shaft when she hit it with her barn-door-size tail.

Unlike Scammon, I had sought to capture a gray whale alive in an attempt to track its migration path by instruments. They were to be carried by the whale itself for a measured period, then jettisoned by radio signal and recovered at sea. I was part of a rapidly growing cadre of whale researchers seeking to understand the living animals in their own habitat—the open oceans of the world.

Whales have swum those oceans, plumbed their depths, and procreated for a much longer time than human beings have existed on earth. The most ancient beginnings of these animals have only recently come to light.

One December day in 1979 an international team of scientists was combing the arid hills of Pakistan. They were searching for fossil land mammals in 50-million-year-old rocks of the Eocene epoch—laid down early in the evolution of modern mammals.

One of the team, Jean-Louis Hartenberger, saw fossilized bone protruding from a boulder. As he cracked the boulder open, he could see part of the skull of a dog-size mammal. The leader, Philip Gingerich, of the University of Michigan, examined it and surmised that it might be a skull of the oldest known group of whales, the primordial Archaeoceti. Gingerich named the find *Pakicetus inachus;* it is considered the oldest and most primitive whale known to science.

The little mammal had probably been amphibious, since it is clearly a whale but was found in river deposits and since its near relatives have been shown to possess both front and hind legs. *Pakicetus* and its kind lived first, perhaps, in low coastal streams that fingered out into the warm, shallow Tethys Sea. Within ten million years, however, an evolutionary radiation of cetaceans—the archaeocetes, or ancient whales—had taken place. Their world was the Tethys Sea, which during the Eocene epoch was a nearly globe-girdling ribbon of ocean.

In Tethys time, the typical archaeocete increased in size relative to its terrestrial ancestors, most of the lineage becoming about the size and body form of modern dolphins. These archaeocetes had long, slim, almost crocodilian heads and pincer-like jaws lined with pyramidal, often serrated teeth.

Then, in a blink of geologic time, a single lineage of these ancient whales, the Dorudontinae, escaped the Tethys and spread widely throughout the oceans of the world. Fossils from this time have been found in strata from the Seymour Peninsula of Antarctica to the rocks of British Columbia.

The triggers for the spread of whales into all the oceans of the world appear to have been the movement of Australia away from Antarctica, a change in ocean circulation, and the beginning of glaciation on the mountainous continent of Antarctica. Its atmosphere grew cold; ice formed and began to coalesce into great ice rivers. Their enormous weight, moving over the rock beneath them, began planing down the Antarctic mountains. Glacial debris dumped into the sea turned the water chalky and opaque. The sea surface froze, making the water beneath it salty and cold. All around Antarctica this salty, cold water sank deep into the sea and began to move northward along the floors of the major oceans of the world.

What could such geologic events possibly have to do with whales? The answer proposed by New Zealand paleontologist R. Ewan Fordyce, of the University of Otago, is that this glacial water was, and remains to this day, rich in nutrients—several times as rich as the usual surface water of the ocean. Wherever this Antarctic water comes to the surface, microscopic

THE KENDALL WHALING MUSEUM, SHARON, MASSACHUSETTS, U.S.A.

THE PAST

marine plants bloom until the water turns murky with their numbers. Then the tiny fish larvae, the pelagic polychaete worms, the arrow worms, the jellyfish, and hundreds of other kinds of tiny animal life find themselves in a sea of food. The sea blooms, fish multiply, the birds in the air above come to swirl and cry, dip and dive.

Such water wells up today along the west sides of the continents where winds press against the sea surface, pushing it offshore. Also, the deep, nutrient-rich water is entrained upward by the twisting surface currents, producing ribbons of richness across and around entire oceans. Wherever this happens, the sea seethes with life.

The initial enrichment of the oceans marks the beginning of a great period of evolutionary experimentation among cetaceans in the Oligocene epoch. Paleontologists complained that nearly every whale fossil found from this period was different. But gradually a story began to come into focus, like a photographic print in a developing tray.

It was the story of a new lineage of whales, the Odontoceti, or toothed whales. Ancient hind limbs had become reduced to mere vestiges, and profound changes began to develop in the skulls, necks, and teeth. From this lineage modern dolphins, the belugas and narwhals of the Arctic, the pilot whales, the false and true killer whales, the river dolphins, and several others would in time appear.

Very early in Oligocene times, probably before the last archaeocete died, another profound split in the new lineage of whales began to develop.

MAKAH WHALING

A petroglyph on Washington State's Olympic Peninsula memorializes the long relationship between humans and whales. The centuries-old image speaks perhaps to the time when Ozette was the Makah tribe's most important sea-mammal-hunting village. Whaling was highly developed among the Makah. Indeed, the pursuit worldwide have looked to cetaceans as sources of food and oil. And whales have fed the imagination as well. Herman Melville's *Moby Dick* ranks as one of the great novels of world literature. Whales may encourage the philosopher and poet in all of us who regard with awe these living, enigmatic "icebergs of flesh and bone."

FRED HIRSCHMANN (LEFT); THE KENDALL WHALING MUSEUM, SHARON, MASSACHUSETTS, U.S.A. (OPPOSITE)

of whales and the bounty they bestowed when taken shaped the society of the tribe. Much ritual preceded the annual hunts. Maritime peoples

THE FIRST MAKAH MEN WHO PURSUED THE WHALES BECAME THE TRIBE'S LEADERS.... ONLY A CHIEF OR HIS SONS COULD HARPOON A WHALE.

This newest branch evolved into the giant baleen whales of today, the huge, toothless mammals that feed by filtering seawater of vast quantities of planktonic sea life, schools of small crustaceans, and schooling fish. Scientists term these whales the mysticetes (Latin for "mustache," a reference to the straining mechanism of sieve plates, or baleen, that hang from the roof of a baleen whale's mouth, and by means of which it captures its food). Baleen plates resemble porous, fibrous curtains. The whale's huge tongue presses the mouthfuls of water through the baleen to sieve out its prey.

By about 15 million years ago the evolution of modern dolphins and whales was fully under way; and by the time the Ice Age, or Pleistocene epoch, arrived two million years ago, the oceans of the world were populated by essentially modern odontocete fauna. The mysticete lineage continued to unfold during the same time span to the present.

Since ancient times people have shared a relationship with whales. The Makah are one example of several Native American tribes that relied on the sea. About a thousand Makah now live at Neah Bay on the Olympic Peninsula in the northwest corner of Washington State. In 1970 a Pacific storm exposed evidence of the Makah's abandoned village of Ozette, the tribe's most important sea-mammal-hunting village. Archaeologists, in cooperation with the tribe, have unearthed harpoons and lances used there in the 1400s. The first Makah men who pursued the whales became the tribe's leaders. A hereditary rulership developed and continued for hundreds of years. Only a chief or his sons could harpoon a whale.

And so it was with many maritime peoples scattered around the world. Such tribes depended on the sea for food; and some, especially those who lived alongside the migratory paths of whales, caught cetaceans. Typically these whaling people knew a great deal about the natural history of the animals upon which they relied.

To this day a procession of gray whales each year parades forth and back along the west coast of North America, right through the domains of whale-hunting tribes—the Aleuts, the Makah, and the Nootka. In the Aleutian chain most gray whales swim through a single pass, Unimak, on their way to Bering, Chukchi, and Beaufort feeding grounds.

Other kinds of whales swim these waters, too. Pacific humpback whales migrate each summer to Aleutian shores, there to weave their bubblenets around the abundant herring shoals. Once Pacific right whales came in considerable numbers; now they are all but gone. So—originally there were plenty of whales for a hunter to dream of catching.

The Aleuts used special hunting kayaks, with a dart man in the bow and a paddler behind. Ashore, the whalers, a special cadre in the tribe, had prepared their gear and performed the essential rituals of the hunt. Roots of

JAPANESE FLOTILLA Oar-driven longboats surround a spouting whale in this 19th-century wood-block print of net whaling by Japanese artist Hiroshige III. Developed in 1677 in Japan, net whaling usually involved crews of more than 500 men. Some harpooned the prey; others entangled it in huge nets.

the monkshood plant were dug, and a virulently poisonous mash was made. Mixed with fat, sometimes from mummies of deceased whalers themselves, this poison was spread on a dart head. So equipped, the hunter pair slid up along the left side of the huge bulk of a whale. With the true hunter's patience they waited their chance. Finally the whale rolled, exposing a flipper. Using a throwing board that gave great power to the dart, the hunter propelled the projectile with its poison into the whale, just behind the left flipper. The dart shaft detached, leaving the poison head in the wound. Then the hunters returned to shore to await the effects of the poison.

The stricken whale might take as many as three days to die. The hunters sang songs in front of a sacred cave containing the mummified bodies of their great whaling ancestors, waiting for the whale to wash ashore.

Anthropologists do not know whether the monkshood poison (aconite) paralyzed the flipper, causing the great animal to drown, or whether the whale died from the direct effects of the poison. Could the Aleuts have known that just behind the whale's flippers lies a plexus of blood vessels that allow the animal to control its body temperature by losing heat to the surrounding sea? It was into this mass of vessels that a successful dart must have penetrated so that the poison could spread throughout the great animal's body. It was, I suspect, the only place where so small a weapon could kill so large an animal.

All around the Arctic world, other aboriginal peoples found ways to capture the marine mammals in their frigid domain. In fact, without them as a staple source of food, such ancient human societies could not have existed along those ice-choked shores.

In the great Mackenzie River Delta of Arctic Canada, belugas come each year to shed their outer skins, just as they do in other river mouths scattered widely around the Arctic. The whales move by the thousands into the shallow waters. There they roll and thrash in cobble-bottomed stream mouths for days until their yellowish outer skin swells and begins to fall away, revealing snowy white new skin beneath.

For the Inuit of Kittigaruit village, the coming of the whales to the Mackenzie was an annual bonanza of vital importance. The hunters lined up their kayaks along a strand outside the river channel. Each was equipped with two slender harpoons of wood. At a signal, the kayaks filed off the beach and formed a line across the bay, and then moved inward toward the whales, the hunters splashing and shouting as they came. The

WHALES AMONG THE ICE
Former whaling captain Charles M. Scammon published his lithograph of gray whales emerging among scattered ice floes (below) in 1874. The photograph of a minke whale in an open lead in the ice (opposite), taken on the Byrd Antarctic Expedition of 1928-1930, appeared in an article on whales in the January 1940 NATIONAL GEOGRAPHIC. It shows the minke's blowholes open, just after having discharged a breath. For three decades the Society has supported cetacean research and reported the findings.

Following pages: Awestruck, a 1937 crowd in Rotterdam views male sperm whale carcasses that washed ashore in the southern Netherlands.

BATES LITTLEHALES: COURTESY OF THE BANCROFT LIBRARY, UNIVERSITY OF CALIFORNIA AT BERKELEY; NEW YORK TIMES & ST. LOUIS POST DISPATCH (OPPOSITE); J. L. BAK / INTERNATIONAL PRESS PHOTO SERVICE (FOLLOWING PAGES)

whales began to flee for the ocean. In the shallow and sinuous channels of the river mouth, some of the whales usually became hopelessly stranded and fell easy prey. Others were harpooned as they pounded their way toward open water. A skillful hunter could take five whales in a single drive.

The captured whales, the males of which reach 15 feet in length and more than 3,000 pounds in weight, were taken to the beach and butchered, the choice blubber and skin, or muktuk, removed and hung up to dry. Meat and other valuable parts of the whale were removed, and oil was rendered and stored in animal-skin bags until little remained on the beach but bones. Stone-lined permafrost pits were filled with the booty, and thus much of another year's food was assured.

It seems that there is no essential difference of motive or skill between the whale hunting of aboriginal societies and that of industrialized societies. The difference was that, in the case of the aboriginals, the catch

ADAM WOOLFITT

was small enough that the whales' rate of reproduction was more than sufficient to replace the numbers taken; while in the case of whaling by industrial societies the opposite proved to be true.

The exact origins of whaling as a venture of urban society seem lost in the mists of history. Early on, it was probably hard to tell an aboriginal whaler from an urbanized one. Both, to some extent, fed the fruits of their catch into trade. Throughout the world's Arctic lands aboriginal trade fairs and intertribal contacts were parts of life long before contact with Europeans, and marine mammal products were prominent in such commerce.

Perhaps the Norwegians began modern European whaling. More likely it was the Basques of the 11th and 12th centuries, who lived in what is now northern Spain and southern France. It was the Basques who injected whale products into the economy of Europe. These brought a fine price: oil for soap, lamps, and lubrication; and baleen—the civilized world's first "plastic." Flexible, impervious, these sieve plates had a hundred human uses. The economic success of whaling propelled the boats of several European nations to supply the newfound demand for whale products.

In this commercial environment the bowhead whale became a rich and prized source. The demand proved far greater than the whale populations could hope to support through reproducing their own kind, though neither whalemen nor entrepreneurs seemed to have understood this fact. "Whales flee in front of the whalers, don't they? Who can count them? The ocean is, after all, vast, limitless.... Who knows how many there are? Who can convince us otherwise?" wrote William Scoresby in 1820.

But the whales swam along the oceanic paths they had always swum. They were not, as the whalers thought, being driven in front of the advancing whaling fleets. The whales' ranks became tattered and sometimes obliterated in the onslaught. In the centuries that followed, whale species after whale species slipped into decline in this way.

One species, the Atlantic gray whale, may have been driven to extinction even before human history recorded its presence. The whale is known in the Atlantic from a few bones, taken from both sides of the ocean, some bearing the scars of flensing knives. This species was probably the scrag whale, mentioned primarily in whalers' lore.

Such heedless slaughter has been the history of whaling up to modern times. For example, when explorers brought back knowledge of islands in the Arctic—Jan Mayen and Spitsbergen, especially—where the waters teemed with huge, docile whales, the rush to the North Atlantic bowhead whale grounds was on. Soon the ships of many nations spread themselves out along the coasts, flensed the whales in the harbors, and towed the blubber ashore, to be rendered in tryworks built on the beach.

Each of the Arctic whaling stations had a limited life span, lasting

COLORED BY CUSTOM
Waters of the Faroe Islands run red during *grindadráp*—"the whale killing." Faroese men put out in open boats and herd small cetaceans, such as long-finned pilot whales, shown here, or Atlantic white-sided dolphins, into the shallows, where they are easily slaughtered. In the past, meat from the kills often meant the people's survival through harsh North Atlantic winters. Although the custom is no longer key to the islanders' survival, the traditional killing continues. Medical findings sound an ominous note, however. Since the 1970s, when it was found that cetaceans accumulate mercury in their tissues, Faroese health authorities have cautioned the people. Scientists worry that the mercury may be detrimental not only to people who eat whales but also to the animals themselves.

COUP DE GRÂCE
Aiming his lance at a wounded sperm whale, an Azorean *baleeiro* (opposite) will deliver the fatal strike. Flensers (right) start cutting up a 50-foot sperm. These photographs, published in the February 1976 issue of NATIONAL GEOGRAPHIC, documented the final decade of the shore-based whaling industry in the Portuguese-owned Azores. New Englanders had introduced whaling here in the 18th century when they stopped for water and provisions. When recruited crewmen returned, they started whaling in the American style, using open boats and hand-held harpoons. The tradition continued until 1986 when Portugal became a member of the European Community—now called the European Union. Its members are prohibited from whaling.

while whales were abundant, and then the whalers moved west, assuming they were following the fleeing whales. In fact they were about to exploit a new and largely independent population of bowhead whales in the austere waters of Baffin Bay and Hudson Bay.

Again, in a relatively short time, that whale population was depleted, and the whalers moved west—this time into the Sea of Okhotsk and the Bering Sea. Finally, the whalers moved north around the northern humps of Siberia and Alaska into the last icebound Arctic Ocean fastnesses of the bowhead. There, it was a toss-up as to who would lose first, the whalers—when they lost much of their fleet in the grinding ice—or the whales.

During the 18th century the slaughter spread from ocean to ocean. Forests of masts crowded Nantucket and New Bedford harbors. First these ships crisscrossed the waters of New England in search of right whales. When these whales became so scarce that no profit was to be made, the whalers turned east and south, toward the offshore waters of the world. They learned to flense their prey alongside the ships at sea, to take the great blanket pieces of blubber aboard, and to render them in try-pots set on brick platforms on deck and fueled with rendered blubber itself. The smoke and stench aboard the ships were legendary, but whalers had become freed from land. They could now go where sperm whales went, far offshore. And the sperm whale catch began to find its way into the lamps of nations once lit by the now decimated bowhead.

Throughout the history of whaling, when a preferred species of whale declined, the whalers turned to the next one, and usually it was more difficult to catch, or less valuable. Near the bottom of the whalers' list was the shore-hugging Pacific gray whale, at best a 45-foot-long creature of thin blubber and brushlike, quite unsellable baleen.

Of all whales the gray proved to have the worst disposition, by human standards. "Devil fish" the whalers called them. Scammon had learned, just as I did many years later, that gray whales would attack humans who entered the Mexican lagoons where the grays bred and bore their young. In his classic account of whales and whaling, Scammon noted: "The casualties from coast and kelp whaling are nothing to be compared with the accidents that have been experienced by those engaged in taking the females in the lagoons. Hardly a day passes but there is upsetting or staving of boats, the crew *(Continued on page 38)*

Following pages: **One day's work aboard a sonar-equipped Australian whaling ship in the mid-1970s yielded five sperm whales. In 1977 the Australian government called for an independent inquiry into the whaling question. The inquiry, established in March 1978, published its report in December of that year, and the government's policy changed in the early months of 1979. Virtually overnight all whaling within 200 miles of Australian shores became illegal; the importation of whale products stopped; and Australia began seeking a worldwide ban on whaling.**

O. LOUIS MAZZATENTA (BOTH); JAMES L. STANFIELD (FOLLOWING PAGES)

THE PAST

CAPTIVE OR FREE?

Hoping to educate the public and learn more about killer whales, sometimes called orcas, Edward I. "Ted" Griffin, then owner of the Seattle Public Aquarium, bought a killer whale in 1965. Griffin launched a continuing controversy when he had the whale, which had been snared in a salmon net off British Columbia, towed in a pen 450 miles to Seattle (right). Enthusiastic crowds greeted newly named Namu, but protesters also raised placards of concern (above). Only two other killer whales had ever been taken captive— one died within two days; the other, in three months. Namu survived for a year before becoming entangled in a net at the mouth of Rich Cove in Puget Sound and then drowning.

THE PAST

SWIMMING WITH NAMU
Photographer Flip Schulke's fish-eye lens captured Ted Griffin chin-to-chin with Namu, feeding the killer whale a slab of salmon. Griffin and Schulke were the first and the second persons, respectively, to swim with a killer whale. Spending several months diving and playing with Namu in Puget Sound's Rich Cove led Griffin to conclude that the animal was affable and bright. His work in the mid-1960s helped dispel widely held ideas of *Orcinus orca* as the "wolf of the sea." Fast and big-brained, a killer whale in the wild makes a ferocious predator for its natural prey: salmon, seals, whales, and other dolphins. But this largest of the dolphins and top predator of the oceans does not—contrary to popular myth of the time and to a warning published in the 1970s by the U. S. Navy—"attack human beings at every opportunity." In August 1984 an article in NATIONAL GEOGRAPHIC reported that research showed killer whales to be highly social and intelligent animals.

receiving bruises, cuts, and, in many instances, having limbs broken; and…accidents have happened in which men have been instantly killed, or received mortal injury."

Some simple mechanical things changed whaling from a venture in which whalers could subdue certain vulnerable species in sometimes desperate hand encounters to one in which they could take the whales of the world in relative safety. These would tip the balance between whale and man—hopelessly and finally away from the whale.

In the mid-18th century Norwegian whaler Svend Foyn began to experiment with a whale-killing "exploding harpoon." It was an awesome swivel cannon firmly bolted to the bow of a whaling vessel. With this inven-

> SOME FLEETS CAME WITH GIANT FACTORY SHIPS AND WITH SWIFT, POWERFUL CATCHER VESSELS. THESE…TEAMS WERE CAPABLE OF TAKING EVEN THE FASTEST WHALES.

tion whales no longer had a fighting chance. Even the swift rorqual whales—the blue, fin, minke, Bryde's, and sei—for the first time became easy prey. In some seas these once unapproachable whales were as numerous as the bowheads had been. But in the years that followed Foyn's invention, their meat, bones, and organs began to enter a hungry commerce along with their oil.

Now even more nations sent forth whaling fleets of their own to join those already there. Some fleets came with giant factory ships and with swift, powerful catcher vessels. These open-sea teams were capable of taking even the largest and fastest whales.

Finally, remote, forbidding Antarctica was invaded by whalers. It was there in the late 1920s that the slaughter of whales began to raise the consciousness of people and organizations ashore. Amid much contention, the message began to be widely heard that the oceans, like the lands, of the earth are finite and that human depredations can clearly wipe out such marine species as we choose to exploit.

In 1925 José Suarez, of Argentina, warned the League of Nations of the impending extinction of whales and called for international action on their behalf. A committee of world experts was then drawn together. The resulting International Convention for the Regulation of Whaling, which later gave rise to the International Whaling Commission (IWC), unanimously called for action to save the remaining whales, and the long, grinding process of reining in the commercial forces of the nations was begun.

In 1928 the American Society of Mammalogists called for the appointment of an international commission "to investigate conditions and facts regarding the life history, habits and commercial utilization of whales, and to make recommendations to governments…as to procedure or regulations which will safeguard and perpetuate this resource for the benefit of all parties interested." Despite the ponderous language, the call had an effect.

The days of these oceangoing hunter-gatherers were, at last, numbered. The human species had turned a corner. The corner had been formidable, and there were others ahead; but this new turning seemed to not allow us, ever, to go back. The whales' long travail began to come to an end at last when, in 1963, at a meeting of the IWC, a group of four scientists— a Norwegian, two Britishers, and an American—finally swept aside industry objections with almost eerily accurate predictions of how many whales would be taken from Antarctic waters during the next season. The result of continued whaling, they predicted, would be, simply, the final destruction of the world's whales.

Between 1920 and 1971 Antarctic waters alone (in planetary terms a relatively modest area of the ocean ringing the southern tip of the earth) had yielded up 307,114 blue whales and 654,367 fin whales. Few blue whales were taken after the mid-1960s, not because they had by that time been spared, but because they were no longer commercially viable. The blue, especially, teetered on the brink of total extirpation from the southern half of the earth, with the fin whale, also known as the finback, not far behind.

The heedless course of commercial whaling was finally halted by the emerging science of cetology, which had started, perhaps, in 1924 when a group of scientists called the Discovery Committee organized its first two-year cruise for research into whales and whaling. Their studies yielded a rich store of information. They learned, for example, what whales ate by cutting open the stomachs of dead ones and sampling the tons of food that cascaded out onto the deck. They measured and sampled the various organs of whales and attempted to calculate the volume of their blood. These scientists developed a slim metal tube, called the Discovery Tag, that could be shot into the back of a whale and later recovered when the whale was caught and flensed. A whale's track could then be plotted on a composite map of whale wanderings. Eventually the data resulted in the first real descriptions of the largest whales—what they ate, where they lived, where they traveled.

From time to time the scientists took berths on the huge factory ships of the whaling fleets. They watched as the giant mammals, floating belly-up with injected gas, were maneuvered alongside, their fluke ends sliced away.

FLIP SCHULKE

THE PAST

They watched as the huge, ten-ton steel grab was positioned over the whale's tail, dropped in place, and clamped tight. Then the whale was winched up the stern ramp, while the scientists were commanded to safety behind protective bulkheads, away from straining cables and winches.

A doctor, R. B. Robertson, serving on one such factory ship, described the chief flenser, waiting as a whale was winched up toward him. The flenser thrust his long hockey stick-shaped knife into the side of the whale as it slid past and, without moving a step, made a long, deep cut through its blubber.

When the whale stopped on the flat deck, the flenser carved steps in its side to climb atop the carcass and continue his work. He quickly outlined with his knife a great blanket of blubber that was hooked and winched loose with a noise like ripping silk. Bones were cut with giant saws lowered onto the whale by cable, and the resultant parts slid through holes in the deck into cookers below. Fourteen whales were dealt with in a single 24-hour session, Robertson wrote. It was from the scientists who scurried for safety amid such scenes that the enormity of the destruction of whales at last became evident to people ashore.

The Discovery Committee scientists began the difficult task of estimating the wild populations of creatures that easily roamed what was to the scientists a thoroughly forbidding ocean. Later, mathematical techniques made possible truly useful estimates of the remaining number of whales. These methods became the backbone of oceanic conservation and of the science of cetology.

FLIP NICKLIN / MINDEN PICTURES; DES & JEN BARTLETT (UPPER)

When I first dabbled in cetology as a young graduate student in 1950, I didn't realize that it was poised for a great flush of discovery. Soon I knew what was being unleashed.

Within the next three decades a radical revolution had taken place. The pioneering cetacean scientists came with entirely new disciplines at their command and with unheard-of questions. They would soon follow the Cetacea everywhere on the seas and into the tropical rivers of two continents. They would discover dolphin echolocation and investigate its almost miraculous capabilities. They would learn how cetaceans dive, breathe, swim, give birth, and nurture their young. And a few scholars would manage to live with wild dolphins for years at a time, learning that they are mammals, good and true, that have taken their complex societies to sea.

During this great spreading time of discovery, I came to regard hundreds of scientists as colleagues. There were two totally different settings for their discoveries. One group of scientists began to use captive partners—trained dolphins, mostly—in research. This work allowed human and dolphin to meet every day in the most intimate of ways. It allowed many precise and penetrating questions to be posed and answered. But it only hinted at the entire sweep of cetacean life in the wild world.

"Captive" is a hard word. It conjures up cages and walls and sadness. But in understanding hands, dolphins can be as nearly domesticated as any wild animal can be, perhaps even definitionally so, since they co-opt human patterns into their lives. Dolphins often become eager, typically (but not always) gentle helpmates, waiting for the morning's instructions, for caresses from the trainer who may love them quite unconditionally.

The other work is done at sea. Usually it is a difficult, painfully slow, sometimes dangerous endeavor, often done on small boats where running for cover from an impending storm or up an ice lead about to lock tight makes these workers permanently wary. But it was out to sea with the whales and dolphins, swimming in their own world, that put into a real-life context the deep partnerships formed between captive animals and the scientists ashore who studied them.

I believe this at-sea salient took force from students of animal behavior working on land. Their discipline had taken them onto the savannas, into the rain forests, even high into the forest canopies, in search of understanding about the lives of wild animals. This work at first was done almost entirely by field men, who answered such questions as, What are the ecologic relations? How do they compete? Where do they migrate? Then women such as Jane Goodall entered the field and took up posts as dangerous and as difficult as any men had occupied. They began to ask questions such as, How are the animals raised and taught? How are their societies built? The animals, described from these two viewpoints, came whole.

At last scientists went to sea to learn the same kinds of things about cetaceans. The main question that long had restrained each of them was simply, "Is it at all possible to learn about wild dolphins or whales at sea when I live in air and they live in water, when I can hardly find them, and when I cannot stay?" The answer was to be "yes." I, for one, succumbed to the question and spent 25 years with spinner dolphins.

With great patience, at considerable expense, and with much wariness about the ocean world, scientists did learn, and are still learning, about the lives of wild cetaceans. So the story of discovery continues to unfold in our own time. And how much more remarkable it has proved to be than anyone dared to imagine. And how much remains for today's pioneers to seek out and to understand.

CELEBRATING DOLPHINS
At the first oceanarium in the world—Marineland of Florida—Atlantic spotted dolphins delight a crowd about 30 years ago (opposite, upper). Dolphins often appear friendly, intelligent, and playful—traits that endear them to people. Karen Pryor, while training the very flexible-minded rough-toothed dolphin at Sea Life Park oceanarium in Hawaii, extended human understanding of how some dolphins engage in a high order of cognitive functioning. She required the animal to innovate a new behavior in each training session. At first, the dolphin's success came by chance; then it made a mental leap, got the idea, and began to pour out new patterns of behavior. By perceiving the context of Pryor's requests, the dolphin discovered that it would be rewarded for behavior for which it had not already been rewarded. According to author Kenneth S. Norris, nearly everything we have learned about the minds of dolphins has come from work with captives. A parade in Taiji, Japan (opposite, lower), celebrates whales as a commercial resource. Former harpooner Hosono Denjiro carries a banner proclaiming, "Big Catch."

DES & JEN BARTLETT; BILL CURTSINGER (UPPER RIGHT); FLIP NICKLIN (FOLLOWING PAGES)

WITH THE WHALES

Haunting sounds from the sea hold field biologist Roger Payne rapt in 1974 as he monitors whale vocalizations off Argentina's remote Península Valdés. With funding from the New York Zoological Society and the National Geographic Society, Payne has spent time here for more than 20 years observing the breeding behavior of right whales. His technique of long-term, on-site research revolutionized cetacean studies. In 1971, while covering Payne, photographer Andy Pruna (above) risked getting into the water with a wild whale. Now scientists and photographers who work with whales often swim with them. As if saluting the growing relationship between cetaceans and science, a right whale (following pages) raises its flukes to Roger Payne, far right; Jim Darling, left; and Gustavo Alvarez Colombo—who represent three generations of whale researchers.

THE PAST

43

DE

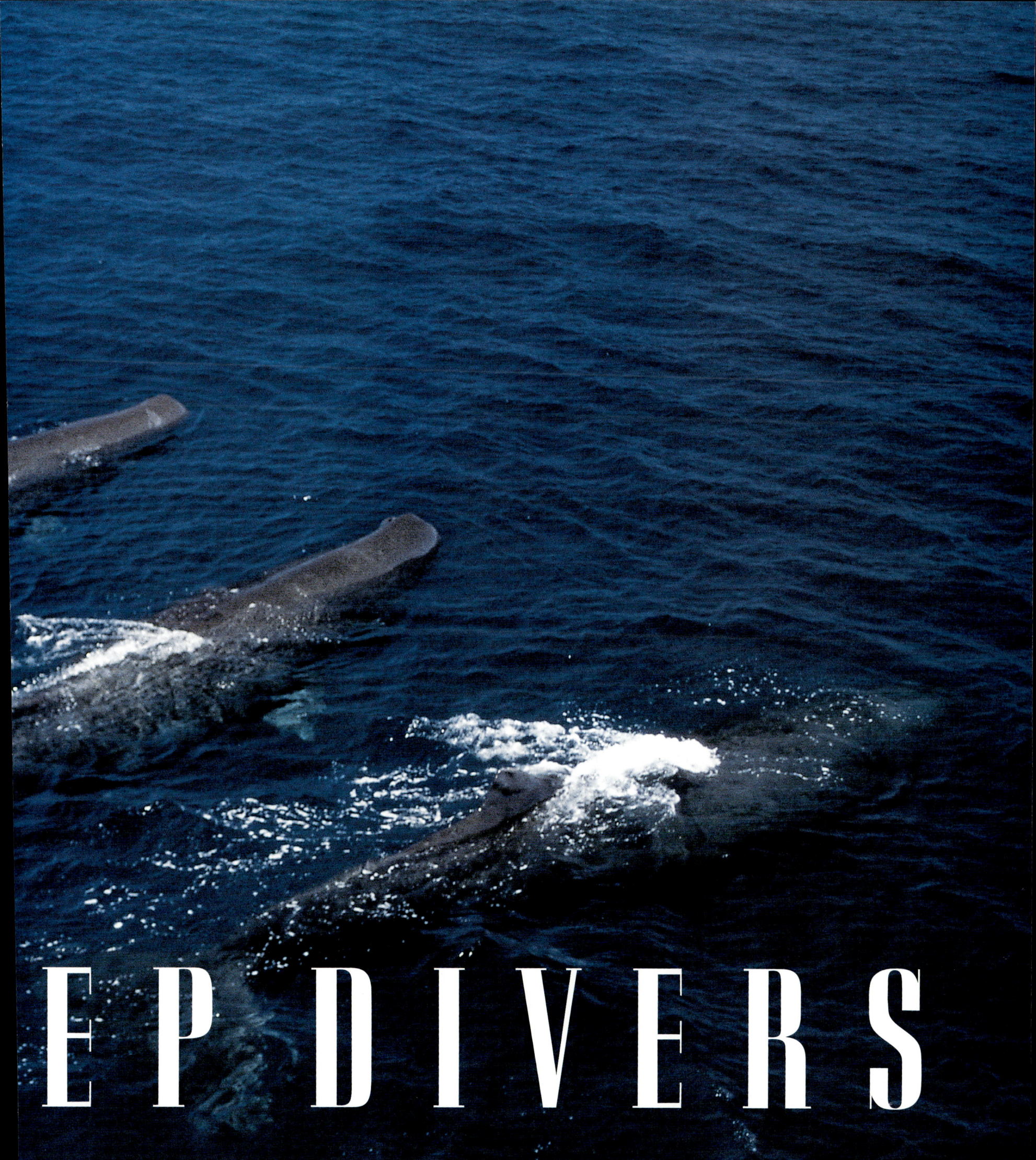

DEEP DIVERS

---- CHAPTER TWO ----

Hal Whitehead

WE SEARCHED FOR THE SPERM WHALE. THE YEAR WAS 1982. JONATHAN GORDON AND I STEERED A SMALL SAILING BOAT INTO THE NEWLY CREATED INDIAN OCEAN WHALE SANCTUARY. DURING THE NEXT THREE YEARS WE SAILED THROUGH THE GROUNDS OF THE YANKEE WHALERS. FIRST WE HAD TO FIND THE SPERM WHALES; THEN WE HAD TO FIGURE OUT WAYS OF STUDYING THE LIVING ANIMALS. WE WERE INTRIGUED BY THIS PARTICULAR WHALE SPECIES, BUT IMPORTANT CONSERVATION ISSUES ALSO MOTIVATED US. NO SYSTEMATIC STUDIES OF LIVING SPERM WHALES HAD EVER BEEN DONE. IN FACT, SOME SCIENTISTS BELIEVED SUCH RESEARCH TO BE IMPOSSIBLE; THEY JUSTIFIED THE CONTINUATION OF WHALING AS THE ONLY WAY TO LEARN ABOUT THESE ANIMALS.

FACING PAGE: *Filtered sunlight dapples a sperm whale as it noses toward the surface for a breath.*
PRECEDING PAGES: *With almost ceremonial dignity, an echelon of sperm whales parades off the Galápagos Islands.*
FLIP NICKLIN / MINDEN PICTURES (FACING AND PRECEDING PAGES)

BABY MOBY DICK

A very young white sperm whale swims with an escort in deep water off the Azores. Capturing on film a whale so rare as an all-white sperm fulfilled, in the summer of 1995, a long-standing dream of photojournalist Flip Nicklin. So rare, in fact, as to be legendary, the white sperm whale was immortalized as Moby Dick by Herman Melville. Contrary to that author's descriptions, we now know sperm whales are shy and easily startled by anything new in their environment. Sperm whales rank as the largest of the odontocetes—the toothed whales. Males of this species have been known to reach 60 feet in length and to weigh up to 60 tons. Females may achieve two-thirds that length and one-third the weight. The sperm whale's scientific name, *Physeter macrocephalus,* refers to the species' head, which typically makes up more than a quarter of an individual's entire length. The sperm whale possesses the largest brain on the planet, weighing in at as much as 20 pounds.

At first, just finding and following the deepwater sperm whales was frustrating in the hot, often rough seas. Several weeks of searching rewarded us with only a few glimpses of loglike backs among the waves.

Slowly we learned to find and follow sperm whales by their sounds. We discovered that we could identify individuals from photographs of the markings on their flukes. Once we could identify and reidentify "Joe" and "Suzy," we could study social systems, migrations, and populations.

When the Indian Ocean study was over and we had sailed back to Europe, Jonathan, now with the International Fund for Animal Welfare, set up a long-term sperm whale project off the Azores, and I started research off the Galápagos Islands. We and other scientists working in locations around the world, including New Zealand and Norway, have begun to describe the day-to-day life of this most strange but also familiar animal.

Sperm whales live most of their lives deep in the seas, foraging in a habitat of great pressure and almost total darkness, an environment we understand less well than we understand the surface of the moon. Their diet is mainly several species of deepwater squid. The habitat of these animals is so inaccessible that most of what is known of many of the squid species comes from studying the stomach contents of dead sperm whales and the defecations of live ones. Of the many weird types of deepwater squid, the most important to the sperm whale may be the histioteuthids. These languid, high-gloss maroon squid weigh from a few ounces to a few pounds. They make easy meals for sperm whales throughout the warmer waters of the world. A more rewarding *and* more challenging dinner is *Dosidicus gigas,* the swift and ferocious hundred-pound jumbo flying squid of the eastern South Pacific, or *Architeuthis,* the great giant squid, which can be almost as long as an adult male sperm whale.

The sperm whale is as strange in its appearance as the animals it eats. From the nose, shaped like a double-barreled shotgun and more than one quarter the length of the body, through the hugely dimpled trunk to the scalloped tail, the sperm whale is built for another world. Mostly, we have no idea how these curious features relate to the whale's life at depth, but in the case of the nose the puzzle has attracted a great deal of scientific attention.

The spermaceti organ is one of the great enigmas of the natural world. The forward part of the skull is bowl-shaped for a sack of waxy oil to rest against. The nasal passages twist and loop asymmetrically around the spermaceti organ, forming air bags at each end, then enter a kind of clapper system at the front, the *museau de singe* (monkey's muzzle). Between the spermaceti organ and the long, thin lower jaw, there is a network of smaller oil sacks—the "junk." Why has evolution shaped the sperm whale's nose into an elaborate receptacle for waxy oil of the finest possible quality?

Scientists have posited many theories to explain the spermaceti organ's purpose, but the most generally accepted is that it aims, modifies, or magnifies clicks made by the museau de singe, giving the sperm whale a loud and effective sonar system. The intense, regular knocking clicks heard by Yankee whalers through the hulls of their wooden ships earned sperm whales the sobriquet of carpenter fish. Hearing these clicks, audible at about five miles through a hydrophone, we found and followed the whales.

Some scientists, however, think that the sperm whales' clicks, powerful though they are, would be of little use as food-finding sonar because squid have no swim bladders or other organs to reflect sound at all well. Kurt Fristrup, of Cornell University, has suggested that sperms may find their food visually: either by detecting prey animals by their bioluminescence—a quality of many ocean animals, including most of the smaller squid that sperms eat—or by looking up for silhouettes against the glow of the distant surface. But surely evolution would not have designed as large and complex a structure as the spermaceti organ without its being related to the methods

BLOWING BUBBLES
Air rising from its blowhole, a sperm whale hovers just below the surface. Toothed whales, in contrast to baleen whales, possess only a single blowhole. The sperm's blowhole lies on the left side of its head, giving it a somewhat asymmetrical look and its blow a low, angled appearance. Appearances aside, the breathing apparatus of these creatures is adapted to handle the pressures of tremendous depths. Sperm whales routinely dive to 1,300 feet in search of deepwater squid and stay for an average of 40 minutes. At times the largest males may dive nearly 10,000 feet to find food. A large bull of this species harpooned off Durban, South Africa, in water nearly two miles deep had freshly caught, bottom-dwelling sharks in its stomach.

by which the whale lives. If not a sonar system for finding prey, what is it?

The sperm whale retains many of its mysteries. But why is this strange, almost unbelievable animal in some ways so familiar? Why is the sperm whale *the* whale, when it looks so different and behaves so differently from other whales and other animals? The answer lies fundamentally in its ecological success: The sperm whale is a great devourer of ocean life. Its extraordinary consumption is partly because of the size of each animal (females weighing, on average, 15 tons; mature males, 45 tons) and partly because of their sheer numbers: millions before whaling and hundreds of thousands even now. Sperm whales have perhaps always outnumbered the members of any other large whale species.

Seafarers sailing over deep water saw many sperm whales. In the early 18th century whalers realized that this animal could be killed easily and that it was a source of valuable oil. Later, during the 19th century, hundreds of thousands of people sailed around the world, killing and butchering sperm whales. The sperm became familiar to readers of Melville's *Moby Dick* as "…the most formidable of all whales to encounter; the most majestic in aspect."

Now, after years of studying sperm whales, I am familiar with the species in ways far removed from the dismembered, oily carcasses floating by the side of a Yankee whaler or the ferocious and vengeful Moby Dick battling his would-be captor. We were initially wary of the sperm whale. After all, it had a reputation for being "so incredibly ferocious as continually to be athirst for human blood." It soon became apparent that the huge animals were even more cautious of us. We confirmed as true the words of Thomas Beale, a 19th-century whaling ship surgeon, who published this description: "[The sperm whale is] a most timid and inoffensive animal…readily endeavouring to escape from the slightest thing which bears an unusual appearance."

We learned the value of treating sperm whales gently, of approaching them slowly and consistently. As we grew more confident of their gentleness, we started slipping into the water to see the whales from beneath. We felt volleys of clicks through our bodies as the whales approached, and then the distinctive shape of a huge spermaceti organ formed from the farthest hazy reaches of our underwater view. The awkward loglike back, which was all we usually saw at the surface, was filled out

THAR SHE BLOWS! Off the coast of New Zealand, a sperm whale surfaces to breathe (below). At such times researchers can identify individuals by characteristics of their flukes. At right, an open-mouthed sperm whale shows its teeth. All odontocetes possess teeth of some sort, although not all sharp like these or even fully erupted. The dentition of some species borders on the strange.

Following pages: **Flukes of a sperm whale spread skyward as the animal sounds, beginning a dive that may take it to depths of total darkness and extreme pressures.**

FLIP NICKLIN / MINDEN PICTURES (ALL AND FOLLOWING PAGES)

underwater into a flexible, graceful being. An eye would watch us briefly but with interest before the whale swept past.

Sometimes as we swam with the sperm whales, we could see them interacting below the surface. One crew member, Gay Alling, saw two of them rub mouths underwater: "They're kissing!" she cried.

There is also much touching, stroking, and nuzzling among these very social animals. The puzzles of sperm whale societies have been the focus of my studies during the past ten years. Who spends time with whom, for how long, and what does it all mean?

Off the Galápagos we track mostly groups of about 20 female sperm whales and their young offspring. They have two principal modes of

WATCHED BY A DEEP DIVER
Cetologist and professor at the University of California, Santa Cruz, Kenneth S. Norris lectures on the magnificent ocean-roaming creature whose image looms above him. Norris and his colleague Bertel Møhl postulated that toothed whales, including dolphins and sperm whales, could make extremely loud sounds, perhaps loud enough to stun prey. Norris now proposes that the sperm whale, which dives (opposite) into a layer of the ocean almost devoid of oxygen—the oxygen minimum layer—for its food, may simply exhaust prey and pick it up. The sperm whale carries its own oxygen supply in its blood and tissues, adapted over time for forays to great depths.

I<small>N THE</small> I<small>NDIAN</small> O<small>CEAN WE SAW THE BIRTH OF A SPERM WHALE. …</small>N<small>OT LONG AFTER, EVEN THOUGH IT COULD HARDLY SWIM, THE CALF WAS ACCOMPANYING…OUR BOAT.</small>

behavior. The first is foraging, which occupies about three-quarters of their time. During this food-finding activity each whale dives 1,300 to 3,000 feet and stays for about 40 minutes, then surfaces to breathe for 10 minutes or so. The group often spreads out underwater, forming a rank about half a mile across, sweeping steadily through the deep ocean, each animal clicking regularly as it searches for squid.

The second principal mode of behavior is socializing. For periods of a few hours, often in the afternoon, the whales stop diving and gather at the surface. As they come together, they may leap from the water, breaching, and their foraging clicks are replaced with Morse code-like bursts of patterned clicks, called codas. The codas seem to be the principal way in which the females communicate with one another.

Lindy Weilgart, my wife and my colleague at Dalhousie University, has made the codas the focus of her research. She has found that sperm whales commonly use about 23 coda patterns and that the different patterns follow one another nonrandomly. For instance, an 8-click coda ("click…click…click…click…click…click….click…click") is preferentially followed by a 7-click coda ("click…click…click…click…click….click…click"). A 5-click coda is often used to initiate exchanges—"Hello?" Sperm whales can interleave their codas into a most intricate duet.

In 1992 and 1993 Lindy and I, with three students and our two children, sailed a 40-foot cutter around the South Pacific, recording codas from every social group of sperm whales we met. Lindy found that sperms in the different areas have different dialects. For instance, whales off the Galápagos favor "plus-one" codas—that is, codas with a double gap between the last two clicks ("click…click…click… …click"); whereas whales off the Christmas and Phoenix Islands in the central Pacific use codas that are shorter ("click…click…click").

Other species of whales and dolphins use whistles, grunts, groans, and other highly variable sounds to communicate, rather than patterns of stereotyped clicks; but the sperm whale, having evolved a system to produce sonar clicks, seems to give it double duty as a communication system.

After some breaching, the grouped females may slow down and, while exchanging codas, sidle up beside one another, nuzzling and touching. Why are the female sperms so social? We can propose several reasons on the basis of our research. Let's look first at how social behaviors support communal care for the young.

In most other whale species that we know anything about, if a small baby whale, a calf, is beside an adult whale, the adult is the mother of that calf. Not so with sperm whales.

Not long into our Indian Ocean study, Jonathan noticed that baby sperm whales frequently switch companions. As an adult escort lifts its flukes to start a foraging dive, the calf generally swims over to another animal nearby at the surface. These escorts are usually older females; but, as Jonathan found, juvenile males also fill this slot in the social order. Individuals in groups off the Galápagos stagger their dives more evenly if a calf is present, so that gaps of time without larger whales present at the surface are shorter than is the case in groups of similar size without calves. The adults and juveniles are baby-sitting the young.

Communal care seems to start soon after birth. In the Indian Ocean we saw the birth of a sperm whale. Within a few minutes of being born, the young whale was surrounded by the other members of its group; and, not long after, even though it could hardly swim, the calf was accompanying a variety of larger whales and even our boat.

This baby-sitting is important. In the best of times, mature female sperm whales have only one calf every four years, so each offspring is enormously valuable to the mother. Although large and fierce-looking, sperm whales do have potential enemies. The most significant is the killer whale. We have seen killer whales attacking sperms. The sperms formed a very tight group, almost touching one another, trying to keep their heads facing the onrushing killers. A first-year calf was safely positioned in the center as the

FLIP NICKLIN; FLIP NICKLIN / MINDEN PICTURES (OPPOSITE)

group wheeled this way and that to face their attackers. The group and their calf survived the two-hour attack with just a few scratches, but the incident illustrates the importance of communal vigilance and defense.

Sperm whales help each other in other ways, too. Whalers noticed that females often would stand by harpooned companions, sometimes trying to break the line. Indirect evidence assembled by South African scientists and some direct observations by Jonathan Gordon suggest that females in the same group may suckle one another's young. Why such a caring society?

Evolutionary biologists believe that there are two general sets of conditions in which cooperation among animals is found. The first, reciprocal altruism, occurs when favors can be reciprocated. It requires that the participants recognize each other and spend long periods together so that many opportunities occur to return benefits. If *we* can recognize individual sperms from their marks and scars, and occasionally even from their sounds, then surely the whales themselves, with their huge brains—the largest on earth—also know each other. We have seen the same females, who travel in permanent social units of about 10 to 15 members, still together after intervals of up to seven years. So there are lifetimes to reciprocate favors.

The other circumstance in which we expect cooperation is when animals are related. Kenny Richard, one of my colleagues at Dalhousie University, has extracted DNA from pieces of sloughed skin that we pick up from the wakes of sperm whales. He finds that DNA markers are more similar among whales from the same group than among whales from different groups. The groups seem to contain matrilineal family units—females spending their lives with their mothers and other female relatives—within which cooperation would be doubly expected.

Richard is also able to sex sperm whales from the DNA in the sloughed skin. From the sex ratio in the groups of females, he estimates that males leave the groups of females and the warm-water breeding grounds at about age six. As they age and grow, males live very different lives from those of the social, cooperative females. Medium-size males are part of looseknit "bachelor schools" found in generally cooler waters than the family units. As males grow, they may venture nearer the Poles in smaller schools, until the largest males, nearly 60 feet long and approaching 60 tons, may be seen alone near the edges of the pack ice in both hemispheres.

Large males—those past the age of about 27—are also seen on the tropical breeding grounds, but we know little about when, how often, or for how long they migrate to the warmer waters to breed. Nor do we know whether they return to the breeding grounds of their birth. However, once the males reach the Galápagos, we can identify, follow, and watch individuals. The males spend periods of weeks to months there during the April-May prime mating period. They move between groups of females, spending about

SIGNIFICANT SKULLS James Mead, curator of the Smithsonian's Marine Mammals Project, studies creatures almost unknown to science—the beaked whales. Inhabiting deep, offshore waters, this family of whales is rarely recognized in the wild. Scientists learn what they can from beached animals and carcasses. Here, Mead holds the skull of a pygmy beaked whale, first identified by Mead's team in 1991. Blainville's beaked whale, perhaps the most widely distributed of this family (skull on Mead's left), like Stejneger's beaked whale (skull on his right) and the strap-toothed whale (skull, left) are known only from a few reports. A beaked whale's jaws hold just two to four teeth; usually only the teeth of males erupt.

an hour with each. No one has yet provided a convincing description of mating, but relations between the sexes seem to be brief.

Even at the height of the breeding season, adult males are rarely seen. Off the Galápagos, for example, only about two percent of the population are large males. Why so few? They are scarce partly because the males wait until their late twenties before migrating to the breeding grounds, partly because only some of them are at low latitudes at any specific time. But humans are implicated, also. In the most recent phase of whaling, large males were a particular target, so even now, ten years after the end of the slaughter, there is a relative scarcity of adult males.

During the breeding season off the Galápagos, only about five large males are in evidence at a time. Occasionally we see two attending a group of females, but generally they avoid one another. How? The "Big Click" may be the answer. In the Indian Ocean the large males were even scarcer than off the Galápagos. When we finally saw one, Lindy heard a powerful crashing coming through the hydrophone: "Crash…Crash…Crash…Crash…."

Once every seven seconds came a sound like a jail door clanging shut. Later, off the Galápagos, Lindy successfully linked the Big Click to the large males. They are potentially dangerous animals with impressive scars on their heads from one another's teeth. Fights, however, are rare. Male sperm whales probably assess the opposition carefully—probably by way of the Big Click—and commit themselves to combat only when much is at stake.

William Watkins, of the Woods Hole Oceanographic Institute, and his colleagues have observed mature male sperm whales interacting with younger males as both appeared to be trying to join groups of females on the breeding grounds. The larger males, with their slow, clanging clicks, were obviously dominant—perhaps mediated by the Big Click.

Which features of sperm whale society are responsible for its members' great success in colonizing the ocean and exploiting its deeper waters? Is it the segregation of the two sexes, the cooperative female groupings, the huge brains, or the powerful clicks made by the spermaceti organ? I suspect that a combination of these factors, and possibly others, provides sperm whales with an evolved ecological dominance of the deepwater habitat.

Elephant seals and swordfish feed on the squid of the deep, too, as

SKELETON ON DISPLAY At Whalers' Village, on the island of Maui in Hawaii, visitors get a bare-bones look at a juvenile sperm whale. The bones, though once covered with many tons of flesh, are rather porous. With water supporting their bodies, whales do not need skeletons as dense as those of most land mammals.

FLIP NICKLIN / MINDEN PICTURES; MARK THIESSEN (BOTH OPPOSITE)

do the 10-foot-long pygmy sperm and the 8-foot-long dwarf sperm whales. The animals with the strongest claim to being competitors of sperm whales, however, are the roughly 20 species of beaked whale. Beaked whales are toothed whales, like the sperms, but the two groups of deepwater whales are only very distantly related. Cetologists were surprised in 1993 when the DNA analyses of Michel Milinkovitch, of the Université de Liège, Belgium, suggested that, evolutionarily, sperm whales are closer to baleen whales than to beaked whales, or to other toothed whales.

The beaked whales—some of them are called bottlenose whales—are the least known marine mammals. Many have not been recognized alive. One species, the pygmy beaked whale, was first described in 1991. Another, Longman's beaked whale, is known only from two weather-beaten skulls. And it is likely that bottlenose whales seen by scientists in the tropical Pacific belong to a new and as yet unnamed species. Three species of beaked whales—Baird's beaked whale, Cuvier's beaked whale, and the northern bottlenose whale—were subjected to whaling. As a result, rather more is known about them, but even of these, only one small population of the northern bottlenose whale has ever been studied alive in any systematic fashion.

The most visually obvious characteristics of beaked whales have attracted the most attention: size, teeth, and scars. These animals vary in size from about 12 feet for the adult pygmy beaked whale to 42 feet for Baird's beaked whale. Only one species, Shepherd's beaked whale, has anything like a standard set of teeth, with rows on both the upper and lower jaws. Females of other species rarely show any teeth, but the males may have two to four in a variety of bizarre arrangements. In males of True's beaked whale, the two small teeth stick out and up from the end of the lower jaw. In the ginkgo-toothed whale, the two teeth, shaped like ginkgo leaves, erupt from a bump on the mid-part of the lower jaw and grow out of the mouth. The strap-toothed whale has the weirdest teeth of all: The male has two teeth shaped like straps that grow out of each side of the mouth, then curve up and over the top of the jaw, preventing it from opening fully. Presumably these teeth are used in the mating process, either in contests between males or during assessment by females. The males of many species are well marked with pairs of parallel scratches, probably made by one another during contests. But the existence of these contests, like almost all other aspects of beaked whale behavior, remains largely speculation. For virtually all beaked whale species, we know little more about their behavior than that they find and catch creatures of the deep water.

Studies of Baird's beaked whales killed by Japanese whalers have led Toshio Kasuya, of Japan's National Institute of Research on Far Seas Fisheries, to think that the greater size of the females and their shorter life spans could indicate a partial reversal of the usual mammalian gender roles.

MONITORING THE CLICKS With his daughter Stefanie in one arm, author Whitehead tracks sperm whales off the Galápagos. Researcher Jenny Christal enters data on a computer. Whitehead and his wife and colleague, Lindy Weilgart, monitor toothed whales worldwide. Their approach to field studies necessitates round-the-clock vigils to record the animals' behavior both day and night, on the surface and below. Fellow scientist Jonathan Gordon (left) listens as sperm whales emit a series of patterned clicks, called codas—believed to be the primary means of communication among females.

Kasuya suggests that the male Baird's beaked whale may provide much of the care for the young.

Clearly the beaked whales contain some of cetology's great puzzles. But how to unlock them? During my early sperm whale studies we had occasionally had brief glimpses of these usually elusive animals, but they were hard or impossible to approach. When we listened through hydrophones, we heard no loud, obvious sounds like the hammering clicks of the sperm whale. However, when I moved to Nova Scotia in the 1980s, the best known opportunity for studying beaked whales was not far from my doorstep.

The Gully is a prominent submarine canyon on the edge of the continental shelf, a hundred miles south of Nova Scotia. It is ten miles wide and one mile deep—the same as the Grand Canyon, on average—and it is home to a population of northern bottlenose whales. This species inhabits the deep waters of the northern North Atlantic from Norway to Labrador. The Gully is the southernmost and westernmost area *(Continued on page 69)*

ALL IN A ROW *Balaena,* "whale" in Latin and the current Whitehead / Weilgart research vessel, sails off the Galápagos with female sperm whales and their young. Typically, females and immature males inhabit temperate ocean waters such as these.

FLIP NICKLIN (ALL)

DEEP DIVERS

TRAILING WHALES

Working the fertile waters off the coast of Kaikoura, New Zealand, a research team follows a sperm whale. With a net at the ready, the scientist on the bow, Steve Dawson, of Otago University, hopes to scoop up feces left by the leviathan. Such details as squid beaks (right) found in feces give scientists clues to the animals' eating habits. Once in the intestines, the beaks act as catalysts in the formation of ambergris, a once prized fixative in perfumes. Voracious eaters, male sperm whales, like this one sounding (opposite), consume about three percent of their body weight a day. A tell-tale trail of stain left behind indicates that the whale has defecated.

Following pages: Risking their lives, Philip Gilligan, left, and Terry Nicklin cut the fishnet that ensnares a whale off Sri Lanka.

SPERM WHALES

As if poised at the edge of the earth, Sascha Hooker, one of Hal Whitehead's graduate students, photographs a school of whales in the Galápagos. With the images the team can calculate the length of each animal. Such careful monitoring techniques allow Whitehead to identify individual animals and study their behavior. Sperms have long posed a challenge to scientists. These whales spend much of their lives at depths humans have seldom gone. In 1979 a tragedy on an Oregon beach (above) gave scientists a close look at the mammals. When 41 sperm whales stranded, scientists attempted to relieve their suffering. At the same time they took measurements of such anatomical features as the sperms' narrow jaws with parallel rows of sharp, widely spaced teeth and their massive brows, which Herman Melville described as having a "high and mighty god-like dignity."

FLIP NICKLIN / MINDEN PICTURES; ROBERT PITMAN / EARTHVIEWS (UPPER RIGHT)

AMICABLE GIANTS
With the easy familiarity characteristic of females and their young, sperm whales nudge each other playfully. This unusual photograph documents the behavior of an adult male interacting with such a group. The gregarious females travel together in permanent social units of 10 to 15 members, with the adults sharing in the care of the young. While some of the adults dive at times as deep as 3,000 feet in search of food, others in the school "mind the children" near the surface. Author Hal Whitehead describes these giants, more plentiful than any other large whale species, as "great devourers of ocean life." Hunting reduced the sperm whale's numbers from millions to a population somewhere in the hundreds of thousands.

where they can be seen reliably. Males grow to be 30 feet long; females reach 25 feet. Because of their reasonably large size and the spermaceti-like waxy oil in their foreheads, bottlenose whales were valuable to whalers. Beginning in the 1880s, Scottish and Norwegian whalers worked their way westward across the Atlantic, destroying the populations.

Ships passing through the Gully during the 1970s and early 1980s occasionally reported seeing bottlenose whales. I was keen to test whether the techniques that we had developed for studying living sperm whales could also unlock some of the secrets of the beaked whales.

In June 1988, the *Elendil*, the 33-foot sailing boat that had been our base for the Indian Ocean and Galápagos studies, made the much shorter voyage to the Gully. For two weeks we explored all corners of the area, often in the fog, listening on our hydrophones and keeping a sharp eye out. We found male sperm whales, pilot whales, fin whales, minke whales, and many dolphins, but no bottlenose whales. I began to think that the focus of our Gully studies, also, would have to be the sperm whale.

We tried again, however, ten days later, focusing our search in the mouth of the Gully, where most previous sightings of bottlenoses had been reported. As we lay hove to in the fog, seabirds settled in the water beside our boat and dolphins came past, their quick blows puffing out of the mist.

BEYOND ALL THE WHALES AND DOLPHINS I HAVE…STUDIED, THESE EVER-SO-CURIOUS WHALES BRING US DELIGHT. IN THE PAST, THEIR CURIOSITY BROUGHT THEM DEATH.

Then, after an hour, we heard a set of louder, longer blows and, to our great excitement, the bottlenose whales emerged. Three robust, gray-brown bulbous-headed bodies circled the boat a few feet away. We tried photographing their dorsal fins and recording their sounds. But photography is hard in fog, and the only vocalizations we heard were those of dolphins. The whales left after a few circuits of the *Elendil*, but they returned later that day and every day since that we have waited at the mouth of the Gully.

We soon learned that finding bottlenose whales is simpler than finding sperm whales. We heave to in a four-by-six-mile area at the entrance of the Gully, and the whales come to us. Sometimes one, sometimes six or

PAS DE TROIS
Three female sperms entwine in a ritual known only to them. With high levels of hemoglobin in their blood and myoglobin in their tissues, sperms store oxygen for use at great depth underwater.

Following pages: A young sperm whale, apparently curious, hovers near Flip Nicklin. For several minutes the 13-foot-long calf filled the camera's lens.

FLIP NICKLIN / MINDEN PICTURES; FLIP NICKLIN (OPPOSITE AND FOLLOWING PAGES)

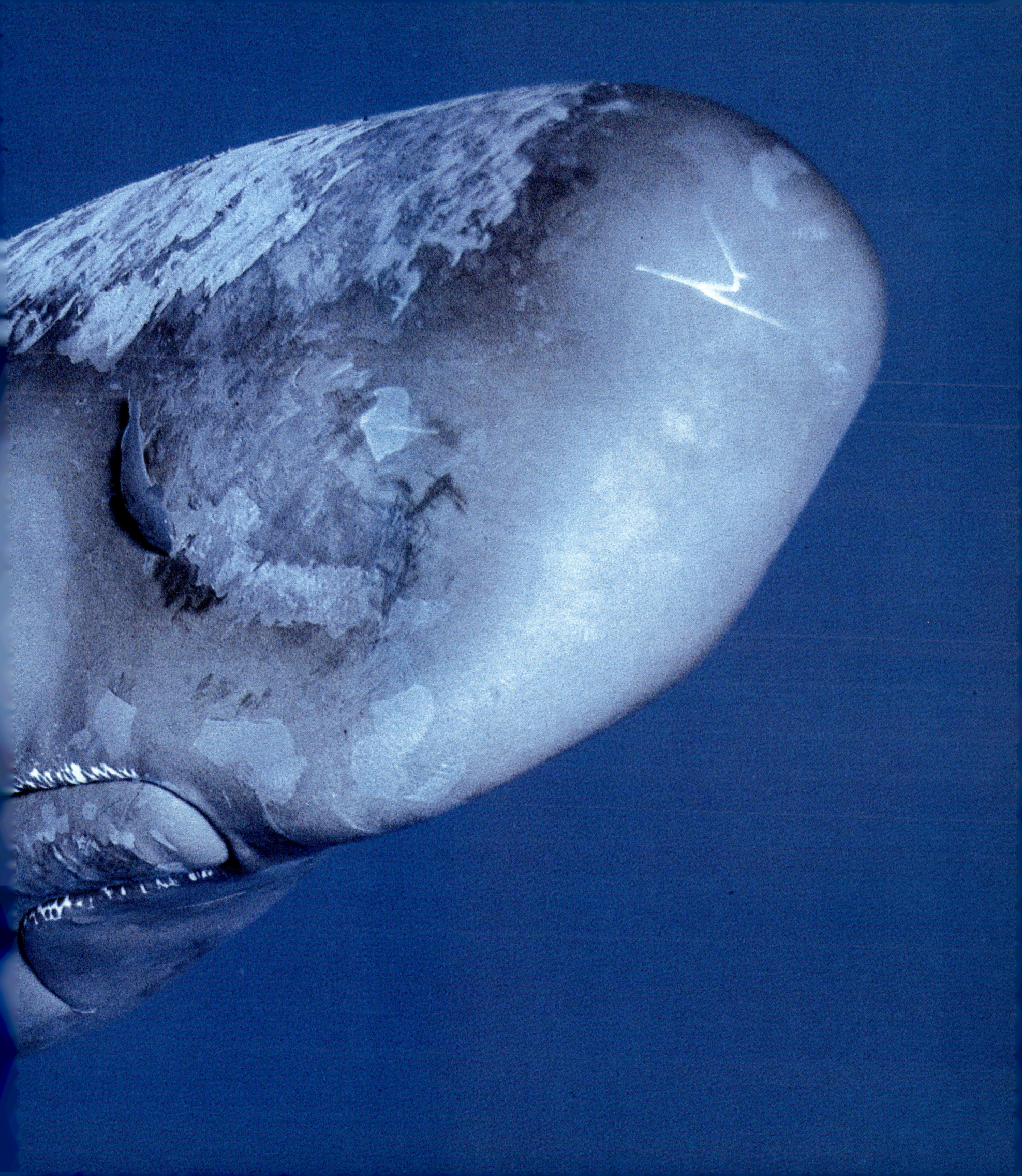

more of the animals approach the boat and circle it slowly just a few feet away. They sometimes raise their strange beaks in the air, hanging vertically in the water, making soft, rude sounds: belches and raspberries.

Beyond all the whales and dolphins I have watched and studied, these ever-so-curious whales bring us delight. In the past, their curiosity brought them death. They were simple targets for whalers who also hove to in areas of abundance and waited for the whales to make a fatal approach.

Every summer since 1988 we have visited the Gully. Annick Faucher, a colleague at Dalhousie University, has made winter trips, also, aboard fishery research vessels. Each time we visit the small "core area" at the entrance of the Gully, we see the bottlenose whales. The photographs that we take as the whales circle allow us to identify most individuals from marks and scars on their dorsal fins and backs. In the entrance of the Gully we find the same 300 animals year after year, in all seasons. There are young whales, adult females, and some large adult males, distinctive because of their frontally flattened heads. At any time about half the population is in the small core area at the entrance of the Gully. The rest? They are probably spread out off the edge of the nearby continental shelf.

The behavior of bottlenose whales is quite different from that of large male sperm whales that we also find in the same area. The sperms wander, seeming to survey large areas of the ocean with their loud clicks. They sometimes pass through the core area of the bottlenose whales, but never, in our experience, do they linger. The small region at the entrance of the Gully, clearly a special area, is left for the more detailed attentions of the bottlenose whales. Without the loud clicks of the sperms, how do they find their food?

Faucher discovered the probable answer when she played at quarter-speed tape recordings made through a hydrophone in the presence of bottlenose whales. Although nothing could be heard at the recordings' original speed, when slowed down the tape yielded loud, high-pitched clicks, revealing that bottlenose whales make ultrasonic clicks, about an octave above the limit of human hearing. Producing these clicks is probably the major purpose of the spermaceti in their elaborate foreheads. The higher frequency gives better discrimination but less range than the lower frequency clicks of the sperm whale, a reasonable compromise for an animal that makes intensive use of an area not so great in size. The bottlenoses' curiosity may be linked to their dependence on, and therefore proprietary interest in, a small area of the ocean.

Despite the obvious differences among the beaked whale species, one characteristic of the bottlenose whales in the Gully may hold true generally: The various beaked whales probably specialize on small parts of the deep ocean environment. If so, this specialization helps them live in a habitat dominated by that great generalist, the sperm whale.

RAREST OF THE RARE
Blainville's beaked whale (above) is hardly ever captured on film. It prowls deep ocean waters, far out of sight of humans. While most beaked whales are hard to distinguish from one another, a projecting tooth on either side of the male Blainville's lower jaw makes it identifiable. The bulbous forehead of Baird's beaked whale (opposite) and its extended, dolphinlike beak are its distinguishing characteristics. An animal sighted in tropical Pacific waters in 1995 (upper) remains unidentified. Cetologists speculate that other species of beaked whales still unclassified by science roam the depths of the ocean.

The deepwater whales appear to be surviving rather better than some other whale species. Part of the reason may be that their offshore habitat is far from most sources of pollution. Their major prey, deepwater squid, are of little interest to fishermen.

But the influence of humans reaches into the remotest corners of the earth. Even the deep sea is polluted. For example, sperm whales washing up on European coasts in late 1994 were contaminated by polychlorinated biphenyls (PCBs). And both sperm and beaked whales die after becoming entangled in fishing nets. Sound pollution, too, threatens these whales as well as other cetacean species. Oil exploration and exploitation, military exercises, and oceanographic experiments are all making very loud noises that can be heard for hundreds or even thousands of miles in the ocean.

Many mysteries and unanswered questions still surround the lives of the sperm and beaked whales—mysteries waiting to be plumbed by scientists who are willing to try innovative research techniques.

To continue sharing our world with the deepwater whales, to have opportunities to watch them and slowly to see into their secrets, we must stop degrading the habitat in which these marine mammals evolved and on which they depend.

Following pages: **In the Gully, a North Atlantic submarine canyon, northern bottlenose whales cavort on the surface. Most species of beaked whales keep their distance from humans, but this species often approaches stationary ships, making the bottlenose easier to study and, in the past, to hunt.**

SCOTT R. BENSON; FLIP NICKLIN / MINDEN PICTURES (OPPOSITE UPPER); JAMES D. WATT (OPPOSITE LOWER); GODFREY MERLEN / OXFORD SCIENTIFIC FILMS (FOLLOWING PAGES)

DIVERS OF THE DEEP

CHAPTER TWO

In the past ten years of observing sperm whales at close range, scientists have come to a clearer idea of how these majestic animals function. But the logistics of doing field research on them, and other deep-diving toothed whales as well, pose problems. The beaked whales are masters at avoiding human detection, generally staying far away from vessels headed their way. In spite of these difficulties, scientists are constantly pushing their knowledge of whales forward. The following facts and theories are part of the current thinking on the behavior of these enigmatic animals.

- THE INTENSE CLICKS produced by sperm whales may cause plankton and other marine organisms to bioluminesce—as they do when they are touched—thus creating enough light to silhouette potential prey.

- BAIRD'S BEAKED WHALE MALES, according to some researchers, may take over rearing responsibilities once their young are weaned, teaching them to dive and hunt. If this proves to be the case, the Baird's behavior would be a departure from that of most males of most species of mammals.

- FEMALE SPERMS SOMETIMES VOCALIZE TOGETHER in a duet of synchronized clicking that cetologist Lindy Weilgart calls "echocodas." She believes the duets could be a form of bonding between females and between mothers and their young.

- THE SHARKLIKE APPEARANCE of pygmy and dwarf sperm whales may be an evolutionary adaptation that serves to frighten predators away from these small cetaceans.

In warm waters off Costa Rica, BBC cinematographer Rick Rosenthal becomes acquainted with a sperm whale that found human company tolerable.

SUBORDER ODONTOCETI

Living cetaceans, order Cetacea, are divided into two suborders, of which Odontoceti—toothed whales—is the larger. This suborder comprises all but 11 of the 80 currently identified species of cetaceans. (See Chapter Three for Mysticeti, the baleen whales.) Odontocetes have asymmetrical skulls and single blowholes, and they range in size from the 4-foot Commerson's dolphin to the well-known sperm whale, which can reach 60 feet. This book treats odontocetes in two chapters. Chapter Two includes the 23 species that exploit the deepest depths of the ocean for their food; Chapter Four contains the porpoises and dolphins.

The classification of cetaceans is an ever changing process as more information is discovered about known species and as new species are identified. Some taxonomists group certain families into superfamilies or divide others into subfamilies. Only families and common names are listed here.

FAMILIES AND SPECIES

Family Physeteridae

Sperm whale

Family Kogiidae

Pygmy sperm whale   Dwarf sperm whale

Family Ziphiidae

Cuvier's beaked whale	Stejneger's beaked whale
Shepherd's beaked whale	Gray's beaked whale
Northern bottlenose whale	Gervais' beaked whale
Southern bottlenose whale	Sowerby's beaked whale
Baird's beaked whale	True's beaked whale
Arnoux's beaked whale	Hector's beaked whale
Blainville's beaked whale	Pygmy beaked whale
Andrews' beaked whale	Longman's beaked whale
Hubbs' beaked whale	Strap-toothed whale
Ginkgo-toothed beaked whale	*Mesoplodon* species A

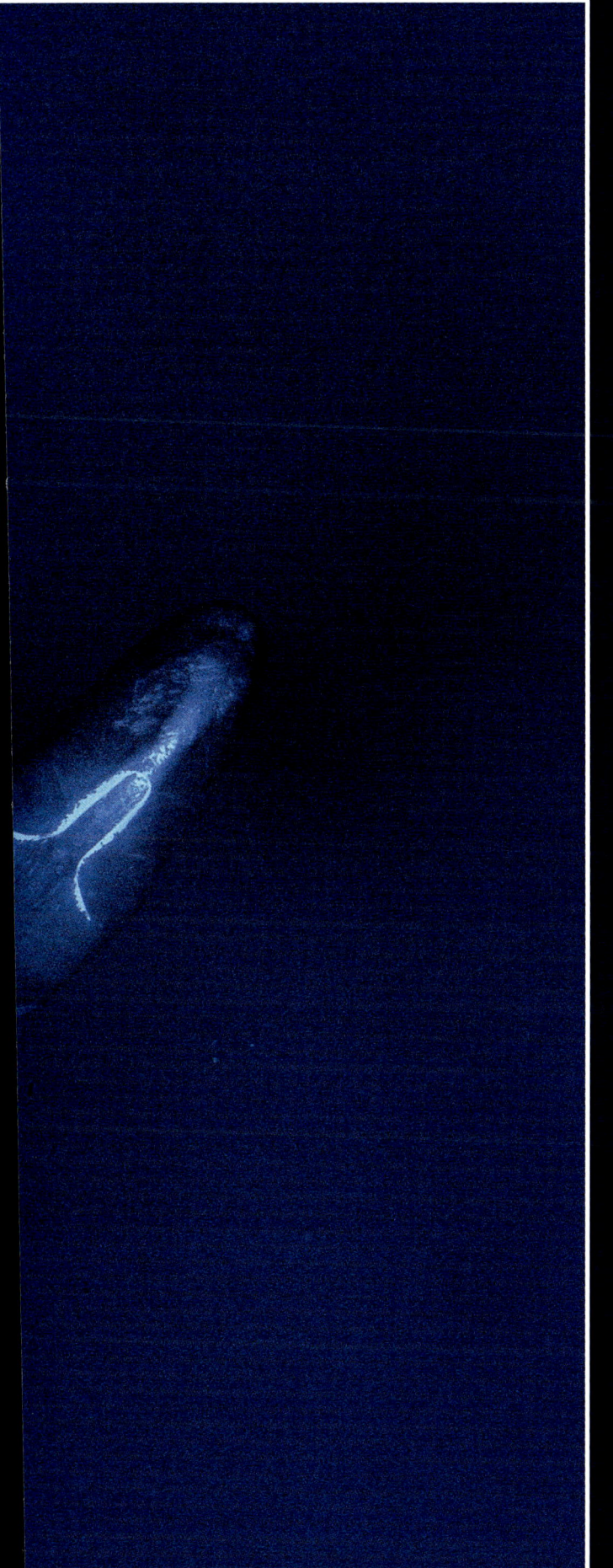

Ethereal image, sperms float upside down, perhaps for better stereo vision or to "lock on" with sonar to the photographer above them.

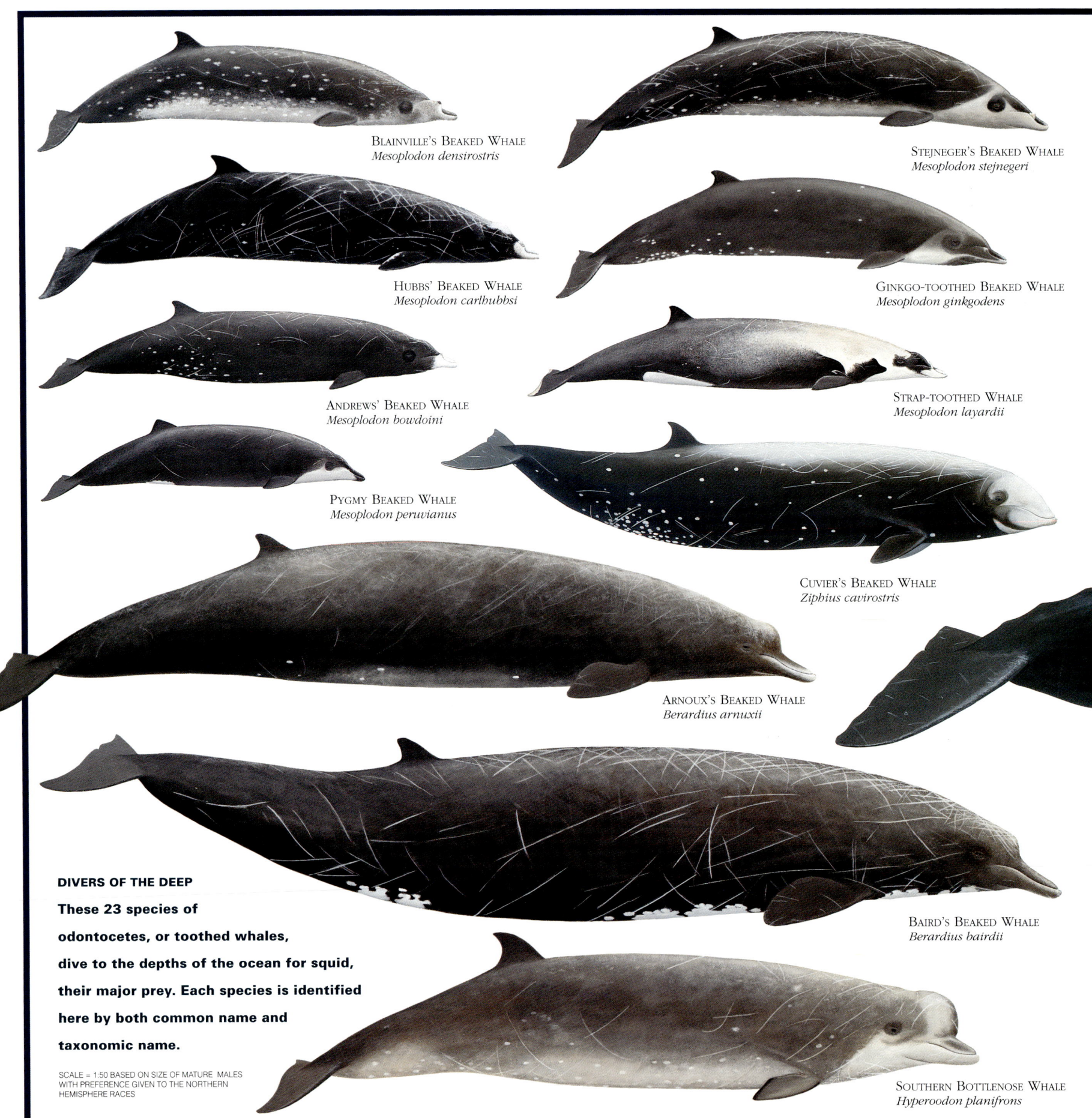

DIVERS OF THE DEEP
These 23 species of odontocetes, or toothed whales, dive to the depths of the ocean for squid, their major prey. Each species is identified here by both common name and taxonomic name.

SCALE = 1:50 BASED ON SIZE OF MATURE MALES WITH PREFERENCE GIVEN TO THE NORTHERN HEMISPHERE RACES

BLAINVILLE'S BEAKED WHALE
Mesoplodon densirostris

STEJNEGER'S BEAKED WHALE
Mesoplodon stejnegeri

HUBBS' BEAKED WHALE
Mesoplodon carlhubbsi

GINKGO-TOOTHED BEAKED WHALE
Mesoplodon ginkgodens

ANDREWS' BEAKED WHALE
Mesoplodon bowdoini

STRAP-TOOTHED WHALE
Mesoplodon layardii

PYGMY BEAKED WHALE
Mesoplodon peruvianus

CUVIER'S BEAKED WHALE
Ziphius cavirostris

ARNOUX'S BEAKED WHALE
Berardius arnuxii

BAIRD'S BEAKED WHALE
Berardius bairdii

SOUTHERN BOTTLENOSE WHALE
Hyperoodon planifrons

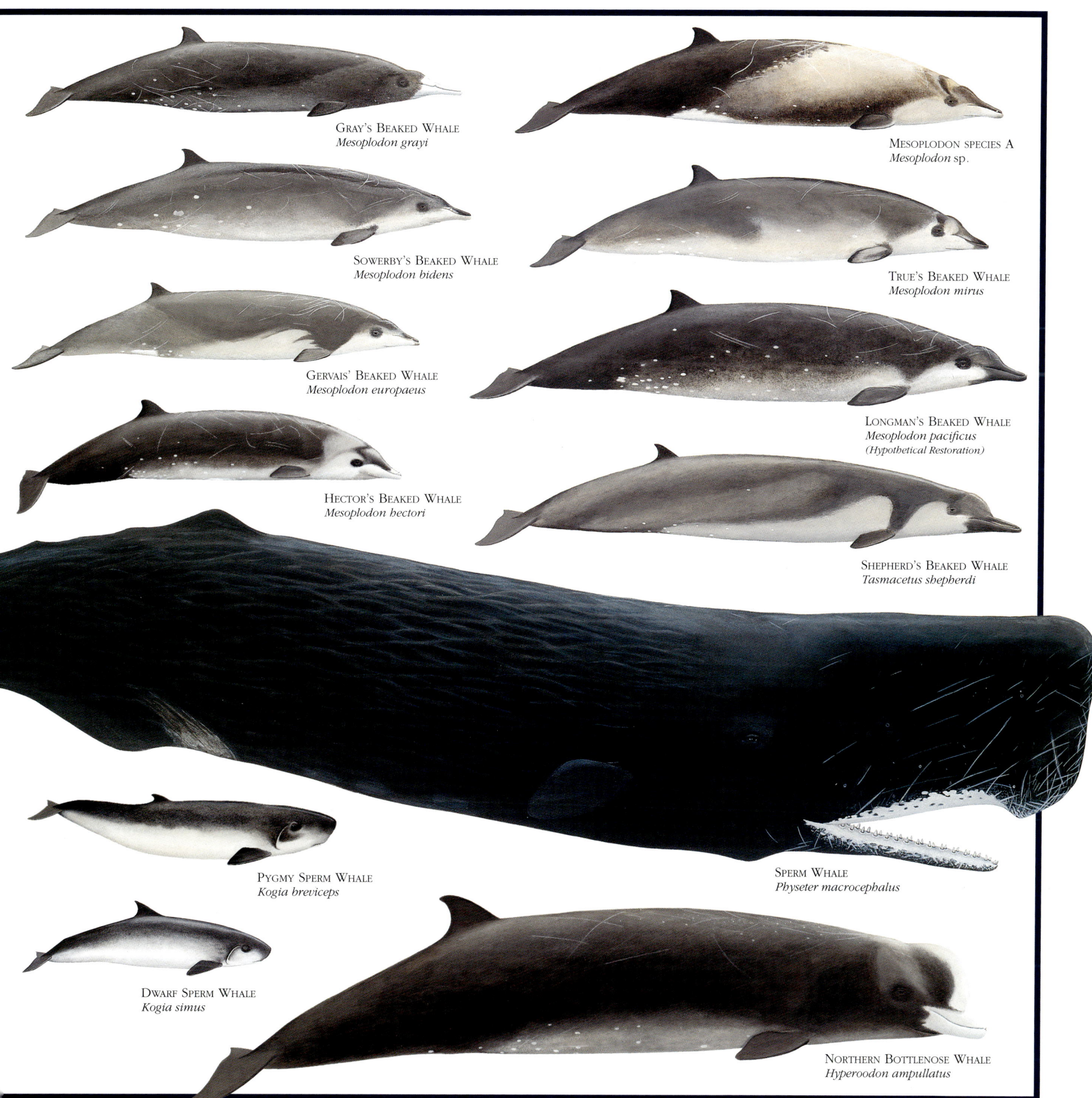

DEEP DIVERS

SEINERS OF THE SEA

―――― CHAPTER THREE ――――

James D. Darling

Early on a glassy morning in a 17-foot Boston Whaler not far off Lahaina we chanced upon a singer. It was March 10, 1979. We were investigating the songs of humpback whales. Colleagues at the hilltop observation station on Maui announced that this would be Whale F, as in "Frank," the sixth whale seen that day. Since 1977 I had spent as much time as possible in Hawaii working with Roger and Katy Payne. Six years earlier Roger, along with Scott McVay, had reported that humpbacks repeat a series of loud, variable sounds over and over again on their breeding grounds—the song. Katy found the song changed progressively over time, with all the singers in one area singing the song the same way at the same time.

FACING PAGE: *Left side of fin whale's head shows dark coloration; asymmetrically, the right lower jaw is white.*
PRECEDING PAGES: *Streamlined minke slices the surface as it sprays from twin blowholes, a mark of baleen whales.*
MARK RUTH / GLOBAL PICTURES (FACING PAGE); STEFAN LUNDGREN / THE WILDLIFE COLLECTION (PRECEDING PAGES)

DUAL SUBMARINES
A blue whale cow and calf cruise in open water off the coast of Santa Barbara, California. "It's difficult to capture on film all of a cow and calf—from noses to tails—swimming in sync like this," observes photojournalist Flip Nicklin. Since 1986, 785 individual blue whales have been identified photographically off the California coast. The rich feeding grounds here are home to one of the healthiest known blue whale populations in the world. It is estimated to comprise some 2,000 animals. "The northeast Pacific is the one place where we feel confident that blues will continue to exist," says researcher Richard Sears. But in the Southern Hemisphere the outlook may not be so bright. Several years ago it was thought that 10,000 to 20,000 blues migrated to Antarctic waters in the austral summer. More recent estimates suggested that possibly only a few thousand members of this species survived in the entire Antarctic region. No photographic identification work has been done there; numbers are based on sightings only. Some researchers now estimate the population to be as few as 500.

Whale song had captured the imaginations of both laymen and scientists. The Paynes had initiated a study in Hawaii to record the songs throughout the winter season and to examine the changes.

The waters around the four Hawaiian Islands of Maui, Molokai, Lanai, and Kahoolawe attract thousands of humpback whales during the early months of each year. The shallow banks and warm waters of the channels that connect the islands are the center of the Hawaiian humpback nursery and mating assembly. It is nearly impossible to glance out to sea without seeing a splash or a blow, or to submerge a hydrophone without hearing whale songs. The West Maui Mountains and the Haleakala volcano often break the prevailing trade winds, creating a lee in the Auau Channel. The calm, clear water allows you to roll over the side of the boat and watch whales—those animals so often out of sight underwater.

Initially, my job was simply to get close enough for a good recording and to run the tape as long as possible. I spent hours upon hours in an inflatable boat, listening. The singers themselves were mysterious, having been observed only once or twice at a distance in earlier studies. Eventually, after much trial and error, in my efforts to get better and better recordings, I learned to locate the actual singer and whenever possible to identify it using photographs of its flukes. By this time, in 1979, locating, recording, identifying, and following a singer through its day had become standard practice.

Frank, on this particular morning, was a pretty laid-back whale. Song recording went easily, helped along by calm conditions and a stationary whale. Frank had a distinctive, somewhat deformed fluke; it was black with obvious white scratches and marks, easily photo-identifiable. He really wasn't going anywhere. He surfaced every 10 to 12 minutes, predictably while in theme 2 of the song that contained 8 themes that year, then dived again.

At one point our boat drifted into the slick caused by the flukes as a whale dives. It's like a circular window that increases downward visibility for a few moments. As assistant Karen Miller and I peered through this "window," she caught a glimpse of white directly below and was convinced it was one of Frank's flippers. It was, indeed. Frank was just parked there, about 50 feet below the surface, head down, tail up, in an angled posture that we would eventually identify as the classic singing position. We grabbed masks and snorkels. Hanging our heads over the side of the boat, we watched and listened for hours. Serendipitously, we had been working with a film crew, including Chuck and Flip Nicklin, shooting an IMAX film on-site. Flip, as it turned out, would later play a large role in whale research. That day the singer, Frank, became a star of the big screen. But—more important—he taught us that we could find and work with singers underwater.

A month later, on April 11, we were following a surface-active group of whales through the Auau Channel. A common sight in Hawaii and in other humpback winter areas is a tight group of 3 to 15 or more whales splashing, lunging, and racing around on the surface for hours. A cow, a calf, an escorting adult, and two other adults made up this typical humpback grouping. The cow and calf were leading the procession, the escort was to the side and behind the cow, and the other two adults followed. The group moved very slowly, without the usual zigzags and forward rushes that often occurred. My fellow researchers and I were again using a decidedly low-tech method of whale observation: We took turns hanging our heads over the side of the boat or floating on the surface with mask and snorkel.

At one point an hour or so into this, Greg Silber, now with the U.S. Marine Mammal Commission, emerged—dripping—and exclaimed that the whales were bashing one another. One of the adults following the cow and calf had rolled onto its side and slashed its tail at the other. They were fighting! This was completely unheard of at the time. A couple of weeks later,

FLIP NICKLIN

AT PERISCOPE HEIGHT
A gray whale projects its head above the surface in a behavior commonly called spy hopping. One eye can be seen just below the baleen. The exact intent of this behavior is not clear, but one purpose is probably surveillance. Barnacles encrust the whale's skin, for a lifelong free ride through food sources such as plankton. Whale lice

(above), unlike barnacles, are true parasites, feeding on whale skin and damaged tissue. Not really lice, they are amphipods, related to those that grays eat.

JEFF FOOTT (ABOVE); JIM BORROWMAN (RIGHT); FLIP NICKLIN / MINDEN PICTURES (OPPOSITE UPPER); FRANS LANTING / MINDEN PICTURES (OPPOSITE LOWER)

now initiated, we saw another, much more frenzied example of the same thing. Suddenly, our many observations of long bubble trails behind these kinds of groups, the thrashing and the lunging, the bloody head knobs and the scars all began to make sense. Adults accompanying cows and their young were not attending "aunties," as had been suggested; they were males competing with one another for position with the female. It was a startling insight into an activity we had been watching for years, an insight that seems blatantly simple now. They were behaving like mammals!

Three weeks later, near the end of the season in Hawaii, Roger Payne convinced me I should visit colleagues Charles and Virginia Jurasz in Juneau, Alaska. They had been identifying humpbacks photographically for years, and Payne figured we should compare photographs. It seemed to me like a long shot. Why would whales in Hawaii swim at a northeast angle to summer feeding grounds in southeast Alaska? The few papers on humpback migration talked in terms of nice, straight, north-south lines. One would expect Hawaiian humpbacks to go to the Aleutians. Straight up. Also, another researcher had just published a paper declaring that Hawaiian and Alaskan humpback populations did not mix.

A day or two later in Juneau, Virginia and I dutifully began comparing my black-and-white prints with their slides, all but convinced that this was a mere formality to confirm that Hawaiian whales did not migrate to Alaska. Were we wrong! Unbelievably, the third Alaskan whale projected was a match to one of our Hawaiian whales. It was stunning. We found six more matches that afternoon. These were the first identifications of whales in their summer and winter grounds in the eastern Pacific and the first by photograph *anywhere* in the Pacific. Our findings contradicted all previous ideas about this whale migration.

A few weeks later when I was in the Paynes' lab in Boston, Katy Payne handed me 11 identification photographs she had taken in the Mexican humpback breeding area. She had recently traveled to the Revillagigedo Islands west of the state of Colima to record humpback songs and had managed to shoot a few pictures. Even after the Alaska experience, it still seemed inconceivable that we would find a match between whales in two entirely different breeding grounds. But again we found a match, further shaking the foundations of what we thought we knew about North Pacific

FRIENDLY GRAY
Whale watchers pet a gray near Baja California. A close-up of a gray's skin reveals barnacles in limestone shells and whale lice.

Following pages: **Possibly foraging for tiny shrimplike mysids, a gray surfaces with a mouthful of kelp.**
HOWARD HALL / HHP

SEINERS OF THE SEA

THRUSTING UPWARD
A gray whale (opposite) launches its body out of the water, turns on its back, then lands with a tremendous splash. Is this behavior an expression of well-being or of frustration caused by skin parasites? Breaching could be a warning signal to other whales. This gray—observed off the coast of Santa Barbara in August—may be summering over far south of the Arctic destination of many of its species. Scientists now know that not all grays complete their classic migration from winter mating and calving grounds off Baja California and mainland Mexico to summer feeding ranges in the Bering, Chukchi, and Beaufort Seas.

Beginning in February, the whales leave the southern breeding lagoons in a progression separated by age and sex, with pregnant females leading the way. Cows and their calves remain in the lagoons for another month or two and are the last to arrive on the feeding grounds.

humpbacks. One whale had traveled to the Hawaiian winter grounds one year and to the Mexican area another year. This fact, to the Paynes' delight, supported their recent analysis of songs. They had found that humpbacks in Mexico and Hawaii sang the same version of their ever changing song, even when separated by 3,000 miles, suggesting that the populations must mix.

It's hard to describe the impact of these events in the spring of 1979. We learned it was possible to locate and work underwater with singers in ways we'd never dreamed possible. We realized that whales behave like land mammals, an observation that seems almost trite now but hadn't occurred to many people then. And, perhaps especially, we realized we had only the foggiest notions of whale migration patterns, populations, and behavior.

IT WAS A TIME FOR SOME OF THE FIRST BIG PAYOFFS FROM STUDIES OF LIVING WHALES, BASED ON CLOSE OBSERVATION FROM SMALL BOATS OR HILLTOPS....

The research epiphanies I was involved with were not unique. Similar stories could be told about the pioneering studies on right whales in Argentina by Roger and Katy Payne, Christopher W. Clark, and Peter Thomas; humpbacks in the eastern North Atlantic by Steven K. Katona, Scott D. Kraus, Carole Carlson, Hal Whitehead, and Charles "Stormy" Mayo; gray whales in Mexico by Steven L. Swartz and Mary Lou Jones; and many others. It was a time for some of the first big payoffs from studies of living whales, based on close observation from small boats or hilltops, identification of individuals by photographs of natural markings, and recordings of their sounds. Most of the studies had begun only six to seven years earlier.

Researchers in the late 1970s and early 1980s had peeked under the curtain of a great drama—"the lives of whales"—that had been playing quite out of sight for millions of years, and what we saw was irresistibly alluring. By 1990 the study of living baleen whales had expanded worldwide. Now the number of researchers and study locations, the techniques, and indeed the amount of knowledge gained have increased exponentially. Before describing some breakthroughs, insights, and ideas, here's an introduction to the Mysticeti—the baleen whales.

Baleen whales have no teeth. Instead they have strands of material called baleen or whalebone, that hang from each side of their upper jaw, somewhat like the bristles of a brush or broom. Baleen filters small food organisms from the water or from bottom sediments. Whereas toothed whales eat larger fish, squid, and mammals, baleen whales eat smaller fish, plankton, and bottom-living crustaceans.

The 11 kinds of baleen whales are all different. In length they range from 20 feet to five times that. Some look like semitrailers pushing bow waves in front of them. Others are sleek and serpentine. They range in color from stark black-and-white to various shades of brown, gray, and blue. Some have coloration patterns on fins, flukes, and backs; one is asymmetrical in color. Some have callosities, raised, thickened patches of skin, on their heads. Some have long, spindly flippers three times the length of a person; others have tiny little paddlelike things that seem an afterthought. The baleen itself comes in widely differing lengths, degrees of coarseness, and color. Some species sing complex songs; other species barely grunt.

Baleen whales are classified into four families on the basis of physical characteristics. One family, Eschrichtiidae, contains just one species, the gray. Another family, the Balaenidae, comprises three species: the northern right, the southern right, and the bowhead. The Neobalaenidae family consists of the pygmy right—the least known of the mysticetes and included with the Balaenidae by some researchers. The Balaenopteridae (the rorquals) is the largest family, containing six species: the minke, Bryde's, sei, fin, blue, and humpback. The humpback is sufficiently different from the others as to have its own category, or genus, within the family. The members of each family have physical and behavioral similarities that differentiate them from members of other families.

You may wonder why there are 11 species and why each species is different from every other. Why not just 1 kind, or why not 12? The answer, apparently, lies in the 11 different relationships between baleen whales and their environment. One of the ongoing preoccupations of researchers is to puzzle out connections between attributes and environment.

Dave Wiley, of the International Wildlife Coalition, has spent time working on these connections. "Finbacks are the only consistently asymmetrically colored marine mammal and are perhaps the only mammal with this asymmetry," Wiley says. The area on the right side of the head from the tip of the jaw to the eye and mouth, including baleen, is white; the corresponding area on the left matches the rest of the body's dark pigmentation.

Much of the earlier literature describes this coloring as a foraging adaptation so the whale could have two strategies for approaching prey. If it chose to present the white side of its head, the effect might be to startle the fish and keep them balled up. Presenting the dark pigmentation on the other side might allow the whale to approach more stealthily. "I believe

PETER HOWORTH / MO YUNG PRODUCTIONS (ALL)

the asymmetry is more likely to have some communicative function," speculates Wiley. "The whale may communicate something depending on the position of the body. If the white patch is proportionate in size to the body of the animal, then it can tell other animals how large that particular individual is and what its intentions might be." This is just one example of the ongoing debate of why whales are what they are.

I've found it useful to think in terms of land mammals and their environments. Think of a watershed in the North American mountains and the different species of ungulates that may be there—moose in the wetlands, deer in the forests, mountain sheep on high meadows, and mountain goats on steep mountainsides. They are members of the same order, but they look different, eat different things, behave differently, and have different social organizations. They all exploit different ecological niches. The variety of baleen whales tells us a variety of ecological niches must exist, also, in the ocean. Although we have yet to visualize these oceanic niches in the same way we visualize land niches, we should expect to see differences in the anatomy, behavior patterns, and societies of their various occupants. Each species has a strategy for taking advantage of the available resources.

Wiley has been intrigued also by the question of why five of the six rorquals are similar looking. "The blues, finbacks, seis, Bryde's, and minkes are the same animal over and over again, just scaled differently," he notes.

He noticed that minkes, the smallest in the series, show a wide variety of feeding patterns and prey species; whereas a blue, the largest, shows mostly stereotypical patterns and an almost exclusive reliance on one type of food. "Finback behavior falls somewhere between that of minkes and blues; and sei behavior, between that of minkes and fins," says Wiley. A body-size continuum apparently exists: The smaller animals are extremely maneuverable and show much more variation in their feeding behaviors; the larger species show increasingly less variation and flexibility as size increases.

Minke whales, therefore, could take on fairly elusive prey in small patches because of their maneuverability; whereas blue whales, with less mobility, concentrate on less elusive prey in larger patches. The blue whale's large size is adapted to traveling long distances, which allows it to search for large prey patches. In contrast, the smaller minke stays in a specific area for a longer period because it can shift food species, and it doesn't have a body geared for long travel and for going long periods between meals.

The ultimate key to understanding whales is to understand the different foods they eat. *Calanus, Euphausia, Holmesimysis,* and *Ampelisca,* for example, are groups of small ocean-dwelling organisms. Although they're not household names, they should be for anyone interested in whales. Food governs every aspect of a whale's life, from shape, size, and color to distribution, reproductive strategies, and communication.

Baleen whales have a full quiver of feeding techniques, pulling out the most appropriate for the type and density of food. Humpbacks may construct nets of bubbles to concentrate planktonic or fish prey; at other times they may simply lunge through swarms with their mouths open wide. Or they may flick food toward their mouths with their tails, a behavior described by Chuck Jurasz among humpbacks in southeast Alaska. Bowheads may feed separately or, as Bernd Würsig, of Texas A&M University, describes bowheads in the Beaufort Sea, they may form V-shaped echelons of up to 14 animals, one animal at the tip of the wedge and others behind on each side, all with mouths agape, using each other as walls so that the prey cannot as easily escape. Minkes gulp herring, capelin, and sand lance; and they engulf krill. Grays gulp plankton, slurp fish eggs from seaweed, or bottom feed.

I first saw bottom-feeding grays during air surveys along the west coast of Vancouver Island in the mid-1970s. Occasionally we'd see whales inside the surf line of outer coast beaches: on their sides in three-foot-deep water, waves breaking over them, flipping around as if stranded, their mouths planted on the bottom, apparently sucking in assorted invertebrates.

It was ten years before a better opportunity arose to closely watch, photograph, and film a bottom-feeding gray whale. Usually grays feed at depth, and visibility is extremely poor. On Easter Sunday of 1984 a gray whale was sighted in Grice Bay, Vancouver Island, a lagoon off one of the protected waterways of outer coast. At low tide, extensive mudflats reduced the water to a few channels. Upon investigation we found a small gray whale, which became known as Quarternote because of a marking on its tail shaped like a musical note. It spent its days in clear, shallow water, filtering mouthfuls of bottom sediments, stopping only to rest and occasionally to rub on nearby shoals. The whale allowed us to hang over the bow of the small boat with mask and snorkel and watch its activity, at times only a few feet away.

Quarternote dived forward, turning on its side like a fighter plane. Reaching the bottom at about a 45-degree angle, the whale plunged the tip of its jaw into the mud and lowered the side of its face and mouth flush to the bottom. Most, if not all, forward movement ceased. Then it would start a gulping-sucking action, obviously expanding and contracting its three throat grooves—an undulating, almost machinelike action of the throat. At times we could see sediment flowing from the corners of its mouth. After

BOTTOM FEEDING

A gray whale bottom feeds, taking in food and sediment while pressing one side of its mouth against the ocean floor and sucking. Water and silt are then expelled in a dark cloud, while benthic organisms remain inside. This photograph, taken in 1993 near Japan's Izu Peninsula, shows an activity depicted much earlier in art (opposite), based on photographs of aerial observations and published in the March 1971 NATIONAL GEOGRAPHIC. This gray whale may belong to the Okhotsk–Korean population, estimated at 200-250 animals. Until recently considered by some to be extinct, this population is one of the most endangered.

KOJI NAKAMURA (ABOVE); DAVIS MELTZER (OPPOSITE)

HUGE APPETITE

A mouth capable of engulfing several Jonahs gathers krill. Throat pleats fully extended, this 80-foot-long blue whale off Islas Coronados near Baja California has just gulped 44 to 55 tons of seawater crowded with the small crustaceans that make up most of its diet. Air bubbles escape as the whale prepares to force out the water in a matter of seconds, trapping the krill inside the baleen strainer rooted in the roof of the mouth. A two-inch-long Antarctic krill (Euphausia superba), prime food for blue whales in far southern haunts, in turn feeds on phytoplankton known as diatoms (above), capturing them in a sieve formed by its fringed front legs. In spring and summer the krill graze on pastures of the minute algal plants that thrive in the sunlit upper layer of the polar oceans. "Krill" includes other small crustaceans such as pelagic red crabs, tiny shrimplike mysids, and copepods. All help feed the baleen whales.

a few minutes Quarternote would stop, turn upright, "chew" by moving jaws and baleen up and down, then—while rising to the surface—shoot streams of sediment from the sides of its mouth, presumably swallowing organisms. After a few breaths Quarternote would repeat the process. When the tide was out, we saw the mudflat dotted with whale-mouth-size craters. The whale had been eating ghost shrimp.

After nearly ten more years had passed, another remarkable opportunity arose in April 1993 to watch gray whales bottom feeding. This was in the most unlikely of locations, off a Japanese island near the Izu Peninsula. There are two herds of gray whales in the North Pacific, one on each side. The eastern Pacific herd that ranges between Mexico and the Arctic is well known. In contrast, the status, distribution, and behavior of the western Pacific herd is virtually unknown. Recent information indicates that an estimated few hundred whales occupy feeding grounds that appear to center on northern Sakhalin Island in the Sea of Okhotsk. In the middle of what may be a migration route of that herd, three grays appeared and began to bottom feed. The warm, clear water allowed unprecedented opportunities for Japanese photographer Koji Nakamura to observe and photograph this behavior. Much of it was similar to Quarternote's, but with novel variations— such as a whale positioned vertically, tail up, head down, bouncing the tip of its mouth along the bottom and sucking in a steady stream of sediment.

Although gray whales are known as bottom feeders and many earlier descriptions support that view, their behavior is more complex than that. Here's what might typically happen on feeding grounds off Vancouver Island.

In late February and March, herring move into the bays and inlets of Vancouver Island to spawn. At the same time, thousands of birds, hundreds of sea lions, and dozens of gray whales move in, following the herring. The whales break from their northward migration, devour the first food of the year in several weeks of intense activity, and then continue on their journey. They apparently strain the eggs off the eelgrass and kelp, or they gulp drifts of eggs several feet off the bottom.

By May most of the migrant grays have moved north, and the Vancouver Island resident grays have moved into traditional feeding grounds. In May the residents may feed on a kind of amphipod, known as *Atylus borealis,* that swarms just above the bottom; then, for a month or so, they may shift to mysids, *Holmesimysis sculpta,* that occur in huge numbers near outer reefs and rocks; in July they may eat planktonic porcelid crab larvae that swarm near the surface for several weeks. By August of some years, they switch to eating bottom-dwelling *Ampelisca* amphipods and become bottom feeders for several months.

Some of the most fascinating feeding behavior of any animal is the bubblenet feeding of humpback whales. Chuck Jurasz was the first to

TRACKING THE WHALES
To better understand whale life, Richard Sears founded the Mingan Island Cetacean Study in 1979. During this longest continuous research on blue whales, 325 individuals have been identified photographically in the Gulf of St. Lawrence, mostly by the patterns on their mottled skin. Sears also pioneered the photographic identification study of blue whales in the Gulf of California in 1983. By matching recent photographs of an individual with one taken in 1970, he proved that blues live at least 25 years. One easy-to-spot whale off Baja California flashes a jagged white scar (left), possibly caused by collision with a ship. Normally solitary or paired, four blues swimming together (opposite) surprised scientists doing an aerial survey off California. "Every sighting adds a piece to the puzzle," says Sears.

FLIP NICKLIN / MINDEN PICTURES (UPPER);
RICHARD SEARS / MICS PHOTO (LOWER);
FLIP NICKLIN (OPPOSITE)

SATELLITE TAGGING

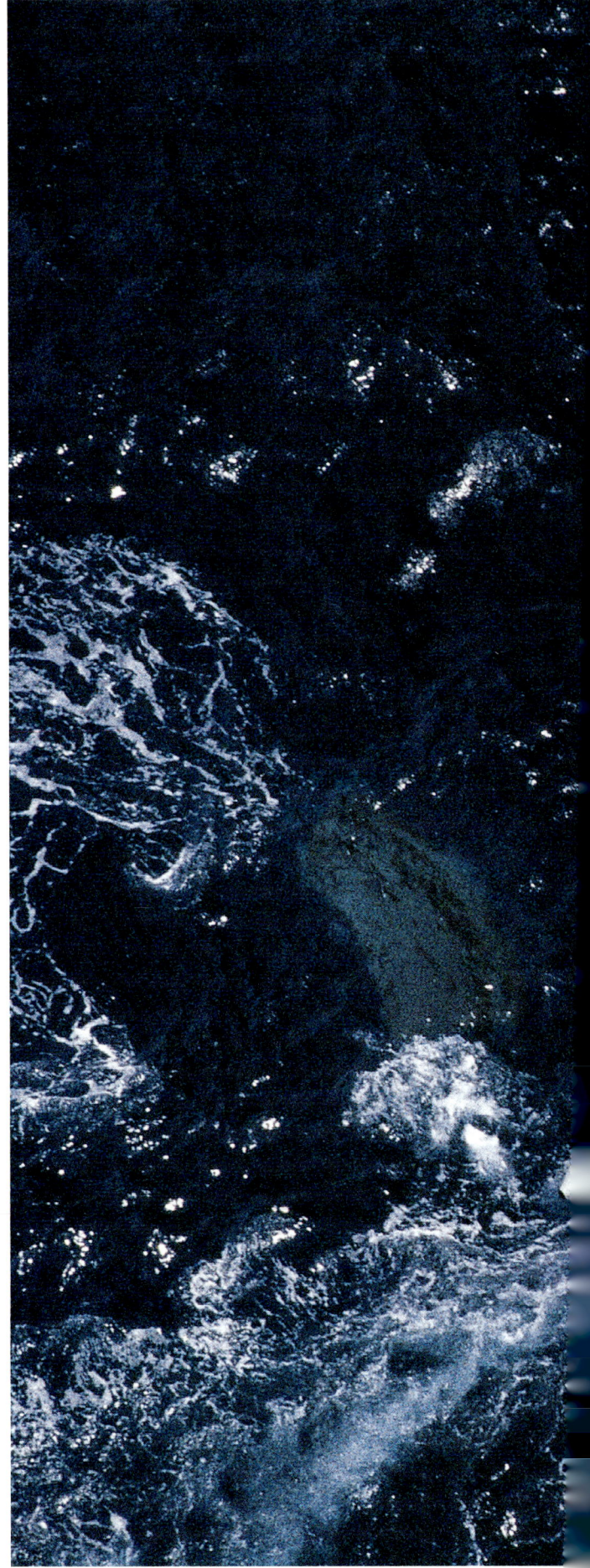

Hunting information, Bruce Mate uses a crossbow to attach an electronic tag to the back of a blue whale. Planted in the thick blubber (right), the battery-powered device relays information to a satellite that returns the data to a monitor on earth—data such as the depth, frequency, and duration of the whale's dives; how often it vocalizes; and the water temperature. The battery lasts about three months. The whale's location is determined by Doppler shift, a change in transmitter frequency resulting from the satellite's movement. The animal's location is better ascertained with more transmissions. Knowledge of whale movements and migrations may add to the chances of a species' survival by identifying its critical habitats and needs. A pioneer in the electronic tracking of whales, Mate waits (opposite) for a blue to surface so he can place another tag. "The extent of whale journeyings astounds us," he says.

describe it. Just about no one believed him. Whales using bubbles to trap plankton and fish? Sure, Chuck! But that is exactly what they do.

In 1979 Jurasz wrote: "A feeding procedure...has been called bubblenet feeding because of its strong physical resemblance to the deployment and effect of a seining net. Major differences lie in the whale's advantages of being able to blow a new net each time, to deploy the net from below rather than above, and to have its digestive apparatus at the base of the purse."

Humpbacks, like other generalists, have a variety of feeding techniques. Bubblenetting is one. Here is the simple version. A single whale works a swarm of euphausiids, the small shrimplike zooplankton often

YOU CAN HEAR A MACHINELIKE THROB, THROB, THROB AS BUBBLES ARE PRODUCED. OFTEN A...HIGH-PITCHED CALL... PRECEDES THE CLIMAX OF THE ACTION.

referred to as krill. After a series of breaths at the surface, the whale dives and disappears. The next thing the observer sees is an 8- to 10-inch bubble, rising and bursting at the surface, quickly followed by another beside it, and another, forming about a 10- to 25-foot circle whose ends may join or just miss. Streams of smaller bubbles follow below the larger ones, creating a spiral-like shape beneath the surface. Once the net is closed, the humpback comes through the center with its wide-open lower jaw engulfing the center of the circle, its upper jaw clamping down tight on the catch. Excess water streams through the sides of the mouth, and the mouthful is swallowed. This will continue for hours at a time. Single whales, pairs, cows with calves—spread over several square miles—are, for all intents and purposes, setting nets and "fishing." We assume that the bubbles concentrate and contain the zooplankton prey, making for a fuller mouth than would otherwise occur.

Then there is the complex version of bubblenet fishing. In this case a group of maybe 8, 10, or 15 humpbacks work together on a school of herring. The group moves slowly on the surface, seemingly resting and catching its collective breath; then the whales dive virtually simultaneously. They disappear for perhaps five or ten minutes. If you listen with a hydrophone, you can hear a machinelike throb, throb, throb as bubbles are produced. Often a very loud, high-pitched call, rising to a crescendo, precedes the climax of the action. Bubbles begin to break the surface quickly, forming a huge circle. Within it you might see a momentary flash of herring as each whale blasts through the surface, mouth gaping. Estimated conservatively, there could be 300 tons of blubber, pink throats, baleen, and extended pleats simultaneously exploding within yards of the boat. The coordination required for this feat is quite incomprehensible, especially considering the fish's capabilities of escaping.

Blue whales, like humpbacks and other rorquals, have numerous throat pleats that allow a tremendous expansion of the mouth to increase gulping capacity. These whales are essentially enormous mouths with tails attached. They gulp massive quantities of seawater infused with prey, then filter the catch. The rich feeding grounds off the central California coast are home to one of the healthiest known blue whale populations in the world.

In 1986 when John Calambokidis, of the Cascadia Research Collective, and colleagues went to the Farallon Islands off San Francisco to study humpbacks, they were surprised at what they found. "We knew we might see blues, but we weren't ready for how many we saw. More blues than humpbacks were present in many areas. We'd see maybe 30 blue whales in a day." Now 785 individual blues have been identified photographically off California.

Calambokidis continues: "Often you get aggregations of feeding blue whales. For example, in the Gulf of the Farallones we estimated 250 blues in a 5-by-30-mile area. When there are dense aggregations of animals, it's often in areas of dense prey—euphausiids, or krill—near the surface. Blues lunge feed, breaking the surface on their sides with throats engorged. You'll often see the water bubble with krill right before the blues surface, just as with humpbacks."

This news of the blue whales off California pleased longtime blue whale researcher Richard Sears, founder of the Mingan Island Cetacean Study. Sears pioneered photographic identification studies of this species in the Gulf of St. Lawrence and the Gulf of California. Both of these study areas are amazing in their diversity of cetaceans. Although the stars of the show are the 650 blue whales he has identified over the last 17 years (325 in each area), the complexity of relationships among the various species is equally fascinating.

When you're inside a large mixed-species group with blows and

HOT PURSUIT OF PREY
A lunge-feeding minke whale (opposite) off the San Juan Islands clamps its jaws shut on a mouthful of small fish. Escapees fall away as the whale exhales a misty cloud. Below, a Norwegian vessel hauls a minke aboard.

Despite the international moratorium on commercial whaling by the International Whaling Commission in 1986, Norway resumed the commercial hunting of minkes in 1993.

STEVE MORGAN / GREENPEACE; FLIP NICKLIN / MINDEN PICTURES (OPPOSITE)

SEINERS OF THE SEA

DEATH ON THE WAY
A harpoon fired from a Japanese whaling ship in the Antarctic arrows toward a minke, the smallest of the great whales. An exploding grenade in the tip will spread barbs inside the animal, allowing it to be winched toward the vessel. Once ignored by whalers because of its size, the minke became the last large whale species to be hunted commercially. Japan continues to take minkes under the controversial definition of scientific research included in the IWC moratorium. In 1994 the IWC made the Southern Ocean of Antarctica a sanctuary for whales, banning commercial whaling. Japan, however, by filing a legal objection to the sanctuary, is not bound to honor it, according to IWC rules.

backs as far as you can see in all directions and with Richard calling out "finback," "humpback," "minke," or "blue," it's not hard to compare these marine mammals with the huge mixed-species herds of zebras, wildebeests, giraffes, and antelope grazing on the African plains. Gray, humpback, fin, and minke whales show feeding flexibility and are able to take advantage of a variety of fish, benthic (bottom-dwelling) prey, and planktonic foods. The opposite end of the spectrum may be right whales, whose food may be almost exclusively the tiny plankton known as copepods. Rights seem to be on a constant search for widely spaced patches of food. They are skim feeders; they swim with their gargantuan mouths open, allowing a flow of water in through the front and out the sides after filtration through the baleen.

Stormy Mayo, of the Center for Coastal Studies in Provincetown, Massachusetts, has right whales showing up in front of his house each March. Fascinated by the animals' mastery of the food supply, he has taken us closer to feeding whales than anyone.

By extensive sampling directly in the path of a feeding right whale to determine the density of the copepods eaten, Mayo found that the feeding environment of right whales consists of widely dispersed food patches that are necessary to the survival of the species. The feeding environment of the right whale has three degrees of density. The first is when the patch of food is dense enough that a feeding whale is actually gaining energy. In the second the food is less dense, but the whale may continue to feed and "cut its losses." The third is when the food is so scattered that the whale does not eat.

"The environment is patchy, and the food is widely dispersed within the patches—but the whales find it. The message to me is that their environment is very delicate," concludes Mayo.

"We know that a right whale will close its mouth and stop feeding at about 4,000 copepods per cubic meter," says Mayo. "Maybe that equals the amount of energy it costs to open its mouth. Below that density of copepods, the whale packs up and goes elsewhere."

The degree to which whales have mastered their oceanic environment to find food is illustrated in the research findings on bowhead whales in Isabella Bay, Baffin Island, the results of more than a decade of patience by biologist Kerry Finley. "Bowheads generally show up in mid-August and reach peak numbers during September and October," explains Finley. "Feeding is the primary reason they're there,

FLOATING ABATTOIR
The crew will quickly dismember the minke whales killed and hauled aboard this Japanese processing ship. Japan is one of several nations that lobby for the legitimacy of whaling, claiming that it is a traditional livelihood and that whales are a natural source of food for people.

Following pages: **Efficient teamwork by two fin whales echelon feeding drives a tumult of small fish upward. Swimming on their sides allows the whales to keep their mouths very close to the water's surface while feeding on near-surface prey.**

MARK VOTIER (BOTH); FRANÇOIS GOHIER (FOLLOWING PAGES)

homing in on seafloor valleys where copepods amass in autumn. In late August, with rapidly decreasing light levels, copepods begin a downward migration as they are carried southward with the Baffin Current over the shallow continental plain. The adults are exceedingly fat. Where the current meets ancient glacial valleys that cut across the plain, the copepods become concentrated. It is here that the bowheads intercept the summer's production of copepods when it is maximally concentrated in mass and energy.

"When conditions are good, they'll feed heavily for days on end," says Finley. "We've noticed that feeding is initiated after northerly winds push the current over the valleys. A south wind will stop the feeding, and

> WHALES ARE EXQUISITE REFLECTORS OF THE BIOSPHERE. THEY LIVE IN A FLUID ENVIRONMENT...EVER CHANGING. THEY ARE BOUND TO...CHANGE...IN RESPONSE.

the whales all come inshore to socialize or rest. They'll spend hours in sex play, emitting all sorts of wild vocalizations and having a grand time. Then the wind changes, and it's back to the serious business of feeding."

Hal Whitehead has shown a correlation between whale distribution off Newfoundland and the wind. "Basically it all ties in with the capelin reproductive cycle," he says. The capelin, a small schooling fish, lives to be about four years old. Each stock has an area along the shore where it spawns. After spawning, currents take the larvae out to sea where they live for about three years; then the cycle repeats itself. Humpbacks prefer the offshore, younger capelin and in normal years are out there with them.

"You know what's going to happen to the capelin population by knowing the weather," says Whitehead. "The capelin larvae drift offshore in July and August. If a northeast gale blows all the larvae back onto the beach, in the next three years the population of the younger, preferred capelin will be down, which will bring the humpbacks inshore to feed on the adults. By knowing the weather patterns of past years, we can predict the distribution of whales off Newfoundland."

Mayo sums it up like this: "Whales are exquisite reflectors of the biosphere. They live in a fluid environment that is ever changing. They are bound, with equal fluidity, to change their patterns in response."

SWANLIKE GRACE
A Bryde's whale shows a pink throat and belly as it breaches off the coast of Japan, unusual behavior for this sleek species. Surprisingly, the stouter humpbacks and right whales leap more often. Unlike other rorquals, the Bryde's inhabits only warm temperate and tropical waters and is often seen close to land. There it hunts small coastal fish, such as herring and anchovies. In this photograph the whale's numerous throat pleats are not extended, making its head look more projectile-like than usual. Whale-watching has gained in popularity in Japan, increasing local resistance to killing the animals. "People are beginning to realize that whales don't belong to any one nation; they belong to everyone," says Shigeki Komori, of World Wide Fund for Nature/Japan. Observing the leviathans has become a major business in North America and in other parts of the world.

AKINOBU MOCHIZUKI (OPPOSITE)

BOW-SHAPED SKULL
The bow shape where the jaws meet gives the bowhead its name. The mouth holds baleen up to 13 feet long, the longest of any living species. Here one whale nuzzles another in Isabella Bay, Baffin Island. Dots on chins help identify individuals.

We have known for some time that whales move in response to the availability of food. Now, with the development and refinement of satellite tags, our understanding of whale movements and ranges has increased rapidly. Less than seven inches long, such a tag has battery packs that last many months. Applied with a crossbow, a tag transmits signals to a satellite. It then returns information to receivers on earth from which scientists deduce the location of the whale from Doppler shift data. A tag can include depth recorders, sound recorders, and heart monitors. Bruce Mate, of Oregon State University, is one of the pioneers in this field. During the last decade, his findings have almost shocked us with revelations of the day-to-day capabilities of whales.

The first successful attempt, in 1983, was on a humpback tagged off Newfoundland. "In six days the animal went 435 miles from nearshore waters to the convergence of the Gulf Stream and Labrador Current, another known humpback feeding area," Mate says.

A 1994 tagging of bowheads off the Mackenzie Delta in the Beaufort Sea showed that "one individual went from Canada past Alaska and over to

Russia, covering 2,670 miles in 34 days." Tagging blue whales off California told us that "they travel 250 miles between inshore and offshore feeding grounds in a matter of a few days, or from Santa Barbara to central Baja California in five and a half days," reports Mate.

Satellite technology enables researchers to observe whales continuously at sea. For example, let's take a look at a mother right whale with calf that was tagged by Mate and Scott Kraus, of the New England Aquarium. Kraus has spent many years studying right whales off Maine and Nova Scotia. The mother whale and calf stayed around the Bay of Fundy for a week, then moved southward. They went to Cape Cod Bay and were seen by whale-watching boats there, then continued around Cape Cod and on down to Nantucket Island and Martha's Vineyard. From there, they swam to Long Island and ended up off the New Jersey coast, then turned around and were back in the Bay of Fundy on the sixth week after tagging. "We observed the cow and calf making this huge circuit within a six-week period. This behavior is counter to just about everything we thought we knew about right whales in the summer months. We had presumed that, once present in the nursery area, they stayed," says Kraus.

"Another whale that really surprised us was Willy, an adult male," recalls Kraus. Willy was tagged in mid-September in the Bay of Fundy, stayed for a couple of days, then took off in a beeline south to Georges Bank, where right whales often congregate. However, he didn't even slow down at Georges Bank. "He kept right on going 200 miles farther, about 400 miles offshore, to the area of the Balanus Seamount. Then Willy went up to Halifax, scooted around there for a while, came around the edges of Nova Scotia, did *not* go to the places we normally think of as right whale habitat there, then down to the southwest corner of Nova Scotia, where he stayed for about ten days. Then a huge storm hit, and the tag was lost," says Kraus. After analysis, Bruce Mate was able to determine that Willy was moving from one area of high food concentration to another.

The movements of baleen whales not responding directly to food supply are geared for reproduction. The classic whale migration is that of the California gray whale, which travels the North American coast from winter breeding lagoons in Baja California to primary summer feeding grounds in the Bering, Chukchi, and Beaufort Seas. Gray whales follow "the shore so near that they often pass through the kelp near the beach," wrote former whaler Charles M. Scammon in 1874, giving us the first description of the migration. Since then dozens of other authors have described this northward parade of whales, separated temporally into different age and sex classes, newly pregnant cows in the lead. This passage of more than 20,000 whales swimming as far as 6,200 miles between their winter and summer grounds has become an icon of whale migration. The deliberateness of it all is hard

HEARD IF NOT SEEN

Their diminished numbers and icy habitat make the study of bowhead whales difficult. Christopher W. Clark, director of the Bioacoustics Research Program at Cornell University, has used a passive acoustic technique to monitor bowheads. With an array of hydrophones suspended 25 to 35 feet below the frozen surface of the ocean off Point Barrow on the north coast of Alaska, he and teams of researchers have recorded hundreds of hours of vocalizations. Inside a "sled-shed" bristling with electronic gear, Sam Payne, part-time researcher and son of whale research pioneers Roger and Katy Payne, monitors the sounds of bowheads under the ice. Highly vocal whales, bowheads emit a variety of sounds. They coordinate their movements through an often pitch-black, icebound environment. Clark and other researchers agree that sounds are key to these and other life strategies of baleen whales. Bowheads number around 8,000 today, reduced from a pre-whaling population estimated at between 12,000 and 21,000.

FLIP NICKLIN / MINDEN PICTURES (BOTH)

to grasp without actually witnessing the spectacle.

In recent years we have learned that not all gray whales migrate all the way north. Some groups break off the spring migration to inhabit home summer ranges along the way. One such range off Vancouver Island is where I began to study whales in the early 1970s. The winter migration there occurs in December and January and is essentially the reverse trip; however, winter conditions make it less observable, and the whales do seem to pass more quickly and a little farther offshore.

In the popular mind, migrations are associated with whales almost as much as is giant size. Books and stories often feature great and perilous

THERE ARE NO BARRIERS.... THIS CONCEPT IS SURPRISINGLY DIFFICULT TO GET A LAND DWELLER'S MIND AROUND.... WHALES CROSS OCEANS MUCH AS WE CROSS TOWN.

journeys. But, as it turns out, the migration of gray whales may be more the exception than the rule. The various baleen species follow a wide variety of seasonal movements or migratory patterns. These range from the long migrations of gray whales and humpbacks to the much more conservative and seemingly more practical movements of blue whales from the coast of northern California to the Gulf of California in winter, or northern right whales from the Bay of Fundy to the coasts of Georgia and Florida in winter, a distance of some 1,500 miles. Bowheads move in and out of areas with the freezing and thawing of ice.

There are no barriers. This is the first rule of whale movement. Perhaps some energetic, thermodynamic, or social factors limit movement, but externally there are no constraints. This concept is surprisingly difficult to get a land dweller's mind around. The ability of whales to move around the ocean basins is nearly incomprehensible, impossible to fathom. Whales cross oceans much as we cross town.

For example, a humpback whale that had been identified in March 1991 off Japan was seen in August of the same year off the coast of Vancouver Island. Japanese researchers later reported the whale back in their region in the winter of 1993. This record is second only to that of another humpback identified off the Antarctic Peninsula; less than five months later it

FLIP NICKLIN / MINDEN PICTURES (ALL)

SCARRED GIANT
A 40-foot-long bowhead in Isabella Bay presents an impressive visage (below) for this first underwater shot of its species. Flip Nicklin made the photograph in 1990 for NATIONAL GEOGRAPHIC. Biologist Kerry Finley (opposite) records whale sounds while documenting behavior. Loud screams and trumpeting sometimes vibrated his kayak, he said. A pectoral flipper dwarfs him as a bowhead cruises by for a closer look. Local Eskimo elders and hunters, particularly Apak Qaqqasiq, told Finley about the bowheads' presence in the late 1970s. Participation of Eskimo elders and students in the Isabella Bay studies has ensured a full integration of traditional and scientific knowledge and has led the community to declare a whale sanctuary, the first of its kind in the Arctic.

was seen off Colombia. This whale had switched oceans, Atlantic to Pacific.

When chatting with marine biologist Miranda Brown about her study of the humpback migration off Australia's east coast, I couldn't help but smile. "We saw competitive pods that contained just males," she said. "The supposed nuclear animal was a male, suggesting some sort of dominance sorting system going on before the males get to the breeding grounds." As part of her Ph.D. dissertation Brown had determined the sex of individual whales involved in various behavior patterns, including the competitive groups. I had smiled because hers was the most recent finding to support a hypothesis I had developed in the early 1980s, as part of my own Ph.D. program. I had proposed that male humpbacks formed dominance orders through display and fighting, behavior similar to that of many land mammals. Since then, significant confirmations and advances have come from research in West Indies breeding areas by Phil Clapham, formerly of the Center for Coastal Studies, and his colleagues.

Male humpbacks exhibit two primary behavior patterns on the breeding grounds: fighting and singing. Singing humpbacks sing until one of two things happens: They stop suddenly and rush off to join a surface-active, or mating, group and engage in competitive behavior; or they interact with another lone adult. Singers are attracted to mating groups by the sounds coming from them: screeches, whistles, and whines, combined with the sounds of one 40-ton animal smashing into another. After joining a mating group, the males battle for strategic position with displays such as tail lashing, expanding the throat (presumably to look bigger), emitting thick bubble streams from blowholes. Gigantic charges and collisions lead to bloody wounds and scars. The activity has all the elements of a classic naval battle. The female swims continually, covering as much area as she

can and thus ensuring that she will attract the greatest number of males to fight it out. By the end of the mating season it's not hard to tell which males have been in the most fights.

But what is the role of the song? A singer stops singing when approached by another lone adult. It had been assumed this was a female attracted by the singer. But the joiners we observed were, in fact, males. Sometimes the two would split apart immediately and start singing again; occasionally spectacular fights ensued. It appeared that the song was, at the very least, a communication between males. *(Continued on page 118)*

**Following pages:
A bowhead's big hello lifts Finley's kayak before lowering it without mishap. The act, although considered more friendly than aggressive, posed danger in icy water.**

FLIP NICKLIN

ECHOING THE PAST

Hunting whales as their ancestors did, Inupiat take a limited number of bowheads each year for subsistence; quotas are negotiated with the IWC. Armed with a harpoon gun, Barrow, Alaska, hunter Eugene Brower waits in an umiak, or skin boat (above), for a whale's appearance. When a kill is announced, the community turns out to help land and flense the whale.

Taking part in an important cultural tradition, Brower's teenage son Frederick stands atop a bowhead (opposite) and slices into the carcass with a flensing knife.

Nowadays snowmobiles are used to haul away muktuk, a delicacy, and blubber for cooking. The bowhead is the only endangered large whale hunted today.

FLIP NICKLIN / MINDEN PICTURES (ABOVE AND OPPOSITE UPPER); EMORY KRISTOF (OPPOSITE LOWER)

SEINERS OF THE SEA

117

I wondered if the song could be a type of display of the dominance position of the male. Could it be the acoustic equivalent of horns or antlers, indicating the animal's size, strength, and fitness? Many questions arise from this hypothesis, and it certainly hasn't been accepted by all researchers.

This knowledge of humpback mating behavior may lead you to ask about the other whales. For instance, how do blue whales mate? We don't know yet. But for a number of years Richard Sears has observed the pairing of blue whales. He reports: "If a third animal tries to place itself between the two, both of the original animals, but especially the rear animal, become agitated and start trumpeting. It sounds like distant rumbling on the horizon. Often, then, the whales will take off speed swimming. Seeing 70- to 90-foot-long blue whales charge along the surface is pretty amazing."

They do this for 5 to 15 minutes at a time. Usually the initial pairing stays intact, but occasionally the approaching animal displaces the one that was initially in the rear. Through biopsies Sears has learned that the pairings are male and female. The female is in front and the male is in back, seemingly protecting his position vis-à-vis that female. What does this mean? Do these animals mate later in the fall?

Sears' findings may be on the cutting edge of deciphering blue whale mating behavior. Some of the elements in this activity are similar to humpback behavior, and both species are members of the same baleen family.

Right whales have quite a different mating system, which includes "sperm competition." That is, male competition occurs primarily during a period of group copulation, and the "winner" is determined both by the volume of sperm and also by the order in which it is dispatched into the female. The female attracts as many males as possible to mate with her, theoretically ensuring impregnation by the healthiest, strongest male.

"When you come upon a right whale courtship group, it sounds like a big washing machine. There's a lot of white water thrashing around, and animals are going in all directions," observes Scott Kraus. "It's kind of confusing, but after looking at enough of these, you realize that in the center of the courtship group is a single animal. With few exceptions it's a female."

The female is surrounded by a group of males. The best position is on either side of the female, which tends to lie on her back at the surface. When she rolls over for a breath of air, one of the males can penetrate her. Whales in these positions get displaced by other males about every five to ten minutes. A courtship group can last for four or five hours.

The female apparently solicits this activity by lying on her back and emitting loud calls. "We've seen males approaching from five miles away at speeds of eight to nine knots, which is fast for a right whale," reports Kraus.

The female makes it difficult for the males—up to 30 of them—to mate. "She swims on her back, turns sharp corners, tries to scrape males off on a boat. We've watched rip-roaring races around our boat," Kraus says.

Only males with a lot of stamina and breath-holding capacity will be able to mate repeatedly. They must frequently lie on their side with blowholes submerged in order to hang on to the female and turn when she does, and they must be able to resist displacement by other males. By selecting for all those qualities, the female is directly choosing males that are fittest.

More than a year after these wild mating bouts, the calves are born. Unlike humpbacks and grays, which appear to have a gestation period of about a year, right whales may take longer—about 12 to 14 months.

ALL...RIGHT WHALES IN THE NORTH ATLANTIC ARE DESCENDED FROM ONE OF THREE UNRELATED FAMILIES.... WHALING REDUCED THE POPULATION TO LOW LEVELS.

Birth and survival rates of newborn are critical factors in the health of any whale population, but particularly for species that have been reduced to perilously low numbers. The North Atlantic right whale is the most endangered population of large whale in the world. Only about 300 are known to exist. The sex ratio is presumed to be 50-50. "However, only about two-thirds of the adult females are actively producing young," says Moira Brown, of the College of the Atlantic, who determined the sex ratio through DNA analysis of skin samples of individually identified animals.

New molecular research techniques developed over the last decade have produced a major insight into the plight of these whales. Analysis of mitochondrial DNA, or DNA passed exactly from mothers to offspring, enabled Catherine Schaeff, of the American University, to identify female family lines among the North Atlantic right whale population. She found only three such matrilines; that is, all the remaining right whales in the North Atlantic are descended from one of three unrelated families. This fact suggests that whaling reduced the population to very low levels. DNA fingerprint

SEI WHALE CAUGHT ON FILM
This photograph may be the first head-to-tail underwater shot of a live sei whale. Seis are not rare animals, but they keep to open ocean and thus are not often observed. Regarded by early whalers as the fastest of the great whales, seis usually travel in small groups of two to five individuals, although larger aggregations can be seen on feeding grounds. They range throughout the world's oceans but appear to avoid extreme polar waters. Intense commercial whaling took a heavy toll on seis, especially in the 1960s and 1970s.

Following page:
If flippers were wings, the humpback might fly. Displaying its characteristically long pectoral flippers, this breaching humpback acrobatically clears the water, despite its huge size. The elongated appendages, early noted by Yankee whalers, give the humpback its scientific name, Megaptera novaeangliae, "big-winged New Englander."

DOUG PERRINE / INNERSPACE VISIONS—MIAMI, FL (OPPOSITE); MICHIO HOSHINO / MINDEN PICTURES (FOLLOWING PAGE)

data suggest that inbreeding may be contributing to the extremely low birthrate of these right whales.

Years of study of individual mothers and their offspring have provided insight into the reproductive cycles and the capacities of various whale species.

"Our first records of Silver were in 1978. She had her first calf in 1980, a female named Beltain, who had *her* first calf in 1985. This suggests that humpbacks can give birth at about five years of age," explains Carole Carlson, of the Center for Coastal Studies, on the basis of her intensive studies in the Gulf of Maine.

Deborah Glockner-Ferrari, president of the Center for Whale Studies, also, has followed individual humpback mothers for 21 years off Maui and has found that most have a calf every two years. But some have remarkable reproductive capacity: "Daisy has had seven calves that we're aware of; four of these were in successive years," Glockner-Ferrari says.

It appears that seasonal migrations occur primarily because pregnant females seek out optimal conditions for their newborn. In species such as humpbacks or grays, in which females come into estrus at the same time, males follow the females. They return year after year to their traditional calving or nursery areas. Probably the best known are the lagoons used by grays along the west coast of Baja California.

Similarly, humpbacks travel to warm, shallow banks in subtropical or tropical waters, such as those around the West Indies, the Hawaiian Islands, the Tonga Islands, or Madagascar. Often mothers with newborn are observed just outside fringing reefs, the mothers resting close to the bottom.

South Atlantic right whales travel to the shallow beaches of Península Valdés or to South Africa and nurse their young in water that averages only 15 feet in depth. Specific characteristics of these sites relative to the health of the newborn are not well understood. Warmth, shallowness, some protection from storms, and conditions that reduce predation appear to be factors.

Young baleen whales separate from their mothers after a remarkably short time. In humpbacks and rights the pairs remain together for about a year; in the case of grays and blues, only seven to nine months. The first few months of a calf's life often entail a migration of hundreds if not thousands of miles.

In their classic study on mother-calf behavior with right whales off

HUMPBACK FERVOR
Two males (above) fight for prime position near a female with calf, as one lashes the other with his tail. Such classic sea battles draw blood on head knobs (top). Aggression among male humpbacks is often witnessed during the mating season.

Following pages: **Courting a mother with calf, a humpback escort sends out a massive stream of bubbles. He issues a clear warning to rivals that he will fight for his position.**

STEVEN L. SWARTZ (ABOVE); MARK J. FERRARI / CENTER FOR WHALE STUDIES (TOP); DEBORAH A. GLOCKNER-FERRARI / CENTER FOR WHALE STUDIES (FOLLOWING PAGES)

SEINERS OF THE SEA

Península Valdés, researchers Peter Thomas and Sara Taber described the early interactions of such pairs. Travel was the predominant activity of both mothers and calves during the entire infant period. Play was the second most common activity of the calf, and rest was the mother's.

Three periods were recognized in newborn right whale development. The first is called the newborn travel stage. The newborn are kept in constant motion by their mothers for the first month of their lives—perhaps because they lack the buoyancy to float without swimming. The second is the calf play stage. The pairs move slowly and erratically, and older calves begin to play. Older siblings may play with younger calves. Mothers often discourage calf activity, perhaps to lower the amount of energy used by their calves and thus reduce the burden on themselves. The third is the premigratory stage. During the last week in the nursery area a sharp decrease in playing and resting and a sharp increase in travel and coordinated movement of mother and calf seem to occur in preparation for migration.

So how do the baleen whales do all that they do? How do they travel across thousands of miles of open ocean to specific destinations, then return to their departure points? How do they navigate their way across polar regions through heavy sea ice? How do they maintain social structure over hundreds of miles or in an opaque environment? How do they find and communicate the location of highly variable and transitory food species? How do they find, compete for, and choose mates underwater? How do they maintain bonds between generations over time? We know they do it—but how?

"The whales have a complete understanding of their environment based on acoustics," explains Christopher W. Clark, of Cornell University, who has explored the acoustic world of baleen whales for 20 years. He is convinced that whales have an acoustic map of their world for the recognition and definition of places, relationships, and activities, just as we have a visual map for the same purposes.

With a series of hydrophones suspended in the water beneath the ice, Clark studied the bowhead migration through spring ice off northern Alaska. He located and monitored the movements of otherwise unseen whales as they navigated the ice. "A picture emerged of what the whales are doing, maneuvering through a horrendous mosaic of ice acoustically," Clark says. Just as he was able to locate the positions and track the movements of multiple whales with high-tech electronics and computers, he is convinced the whales do the same, listening to acoustic cues from the surrounding environment and figuring out what's going on and where they are.

According to Clark, "The whales were approaching this massive ice floe. The whales in the lead, the scouts, increased their call rate as they got closer. When they were about half a mile from the ice, they dramatically increased how often they called, as they began to detour around it."

BUBBLES ABOUND
A humpback calf moves above a cow as she is gently caressed by bubbles blown by a male (opposite). The adults swam away together, then rejoined the youngster nearly 15 minutes later. A lone male (below) assumes the angled, head-down posture of humpback singers. Hanging motionless within 150 feet of the surface, with flippers outstretched, males perform precise and haunting arias. The elaborate songs may be a male dominance display.

FLIP NICKLIN / MINDEN PICTURES; FLIP NICKLIN (OPPOSITE)

CLOSE ENCOUNTERS

For hands-on experience with wild whales, it's hard to top Argentina's Península Valdés. Researchers come here because southern right whales converge offshore every austral winter to mate and to bear young. When Flip Nicklin and Argentine researcher David Garciarena took to the water to approach a mother and calf (above), the 15-foot-long youngster readily drew near enough to fill Nicklin's 16-mm, wide-angle lens (far right). "Like a big puppy," the photographer recalls. Years earlier, underwater photographers first swam with whales in these same waters. Bill Curtsinger's close encounter with a 50-ton adult at Valdés yielded an evocative display of departing flukes (below).

WHALES

FLIP NICKLIN; ROGER PAYNE / WHALE CONSERVATION INSTITUTE (OPPOSITE UPPER); BILL CURTSINGER (OPPOSITE)

SEINERS OF THE SEA

127

Followers nearly a mile behind the scouts must have been listening either to the changing location of the leaders' voices or to the echoes of the leaders' calls off the ice. They began the detour while farther away from the ice than the leaders had been when *they* started detouring.

We now recognize that sounds, both those made by themselves and those coming from their environment, are key to the life strategies of baleen whales. They seem to use calls to identify an individual, its location, and its emotion. Baleen species use sounds to different degrees and in different ways. Grays apparently have a smaller vocal repertoire than rights, humpbacks, and bowheads. Some species have complex acoustic displays, as in the humpbacks' song. The bowhead, also, repeats sounds in the form of song. Blues and finbacks produce loud low-frequency calls, often below the range of human hearing, that travel great distances in the right conditions.

WARTY APPARITION Off Argentina's Península Valdés, a right whale raises the top of its head and open mouth above water. The rough callosities, brightly colored by whale lice, help serve as identification markers for researchers.

FLIP NICKLIN / MINDEN PICTURES (ALL)

Insights into the acoustic world of baleen whales have exploded since 1992, when the U.S. Navy opened up the doors to its sophisticated underwater listening stations developed to track submarines. The Navy engaged Clark to help evaluate the system for detecting, locating, and tracking whales. "The initial results were nothing short of extraordinary," says Clark. Sound recordings obtained from hydrophone arrays on the floor of the Atlantic indicated how low-frequency, passive acoustics—listening for whale calls—can be used to describe large-scale seasonal distributions, movements, and the relative abundance of deepwater whales. In the first nine months, many tens of thousands of blue, finback, humpback, and minke whale calls were heard; many hundreds of animals were located; and many tens of individuals were tracked for periods ranging from a few hours to many weeks.

THE ABILITY TO FOLLOW INDIVIDUAL WHALES ACROSS ENTIRE OCEAN BASINS BY SIMPLY LISTENING TO THEM VERGES ON WHAT USED TO SEEM LIKE SCIENCE FICTION.

The enormous potential for the benign use of the Integrated Undersea Surveillance System is hinted at with the story of Ol' Blue, a blue whale passively detected by Navy analyst Chuck Gagnon. Gagnon tracked it by the thousands of calls it emitted—sounds that resulted in a sonic fingerprint used to differentiate Ol' Blue from other blues during 43 days as it traveled 1,700 nautical miles. It moved from a position northeast of Bermuda to a point 200 nautical miles northeast of the Bahamas before returning north.

The ability to follow individual whales across entire ocean basins by simply listening to them verges on what used to seem like science fiction. Also the fact that whales broadcast low-frequency sounds over thousands of miles may seem stranger than fiction. When Roger Payne proposed that concept in the early 1970s, it was beyond the comprehension of most people. Now we know that some whales do it all the time.

The knowledge we have gained of baleen whales has changed forever the way we view them. The ocean basins are their backyard, and their acoustic systems are perfectly suited for communication, navigation, reproduction, and food finding within the vast, deep spaces they call home.

LASAGNA TAIL
Named for scallops at the end of its tail (above), a calf signals feeding time (upper). The young right whale lays its flukes over its dozing mother's blowhole to get attention. Cows at times restrain frolicsome calves with their pectoral flippers.

Following pages: Whale of a tail, a right's 20-foot-wide flukes drape above the sea as it dives to its underwater realm.

DES & JEN BARTLETT (FOLLOWING PAGES)

SEINERS OF THE SEA

BALEEN WHALES

CHAPTER THREE

Baleen whales include the largest of all living animals—the blue whale. This species is also the largest ever to have lived on earth, exceeding in size even the largest dinosaurs. Alarming reductions of baleen whales are attributable to human activities. They have been imperiled first by overhunting and now by degradation of their habitat. The demands of humans for food from the seas may threaten the whales' nutrition. Although the hunting of baleen whales has declined, scientists are concerned about the slow repopulation of some species. Scientists move one step closer toward aiding the whales' recovery to truly viable numbers with each detail of their hidden lives they discover.

● WHALES behave in ways similar to land mammals; social and behavioral characteristics have been modified for life in a liquid environment.

● DIFFERENCES AMONG THE SPECIES ultimately relate to the different ecological niches they inhabit within the oceans.

● SOME BALEEN WHALES may travel over entire ocean basins, and even between oceans, in just a matter of months.

● VOCAL REPERTOIRES vary from complex and ever changing songs to simple grunts. Whales navigate by means of acoustics.

● THE STATUS OF POPULATIONS varies from "near pre-whaling levels" to "critically endangered."

A gulp 13 feet wide by a feeding humpback whale exposes the bony pink roof of the mouth, from which grows the food-entrapping sieve of baleen.

SEINERS OF THE SEA

SUBORDER MYSTICETI

Members of the suborder Mysticeti, or mysticetes, are baleen whales. The term "mysticete" derives from the Latin for "mustache," a reference to the baleen, a fibrous curtain of material growing from the upper jaw of all members of this suborder. Baleen ranges in length and texture from the 15-inch coarse bristles of gray whales to the 13-foot horsehair-like fringe of bowheads. Mysticetes differ from odontocetes, or toothed whales (treated in Chapters Two and Four), in several ways. The most obvious difference is the mysticetes' lack of teeth: They use baleen, instead, to trap the plankton, crustaceans, and small fish that make up their diets. Other differences include the symmetrical skulls of baleen whales and their paired nostrils, or blowholes.

The 11 species of mysticetes exploit different ecological niches in the ocean and exhibit a wide variety of behavioral patterns and anatomical features. They range in size from the relatively small pygmy right whale, about 18 feet long, to the blue whale, which can measure 90 feet in length. Despite their considerable size, mysticetes consume some of the ocean's smallest organisms.

Note: Not all scientists agree that the pygmy right whale should be classified as a separate family, but in the minds of many it is different enough from other right whale species to warrant this distinction.

FAMILIES AND SPECIES

Family Eschrichtiidae

Gray whale

Family Balaenidae

Northern right whale	Bowhead whale
Southern right whale	

Family Neobalaenidae

Pygmy right whale

Family Balaenopteridae

Minke whale	Fin whale
Bryde's whale	Blue whale
Sei whale	Humpback whale

Bottlenose dolphins swim with a humpback cow and calf, not an unusual sight off the west coast of Maui.

BOWHEAD WHALE
Balaena mysticetus

NORTHERN RIGHT WHALE
Eubalaena glacialis

PYGMY RIGHT WHALE
Caperea marginata

GRAY WHALE
Eschrichtius robustus

BALEEN WHALES

Eleven species of mysticetes exploit different ecological niches of the ocean. They vary in looks and behavior, but all possess baleen instead of teeth.

SCALE=1:70 BASED ON SIZE OF MATURE MALES WITH PREFERENCE GIVEN TO THE NORTHERN HEMISPHERE RACES

BRYDE'S WHALE
Balaenoptera edeni

SEI WHALE
Balaenoptera borealis

SEINERS OF THE SEA

REALM OF

REALM OF DOLPHINS

---------- CHAPTER FOUR ----------

Bernd Würsig

When I cast my mind back to the most thrilling marine mammal experiences of my life, one episode— my very first with dolphins—stands out. I had just labored to get into a tight, uncomfortable wet suit, tugging and pulling while growing slightly nauseous in a tossing rubber raft. Then I was underwater, head cleared by the sudden cold, free diving with only mask, snorkel, and flippers in the green, plankton-rich waters off Patagonia, southern Argentina. Out of the gloom came streamlined, black-nosed, darting shapes: dusky dolphins. They whirled around me once or twice, then were gone. Again and again more dolphins came, each taking time to quickly check out this stranger

FACING PAGE: *Its head seemingly in the clouds, a bottlenose dolphin navigates through reflected sky.*
PRECEDING PAGES: *Brothers in the brine, Atlantic spotted dolphins converse in whistles.*
DAVID DOUBILET (FACING PAGE); FLIP NICKLIN (PRECEDING PAGES)

**NURSERY IN THE BLUE
Birthing and nursing underwater demands specialized equipment for resident mammals, such as this pilot whale suckling her calf off Hawaii. As with other streamlined members of the family Delphinidae, the nipple lies protected within a mammary slit, protruding only during nursing. Muscles force milk into the calf's mouth, shortening feeding time. Most pilot whales nurse young about 20 months, but some offspring continue suckling even after taking solid food, at times for up to 15 years. All dolphins share sonar capabilities; clicks sent from their bulging foreheads reflect off underwater objects and return, enabling the animals to define their realm. A gregarious species, pilot whales live in pods of up to a hundred or more individuals, and endure for many years. Their cohesiveness can lead to mass mortality; coastal whalers herd groups into shallows to be killed. Pilot whales also strand themselves on beaches, for reasons we poorly understand.**

in their world—and then go about their business. They scanned me not only with eyes, but also with what I felt in my head as a rapid buzz of clicks; they were echolocating, "seeing" me by sound as well as by sight. These were wild animals, roughly my size, and yet they came so close, with no fear or aggression. I, too, felt no fear, only exhilaration; there was nothing in the movements of these sleek mammals to give alarm.

It all happened on a spring morning in the Southern Hemisphere a quarter of a century ago. I was a beginning graduate student, truly ignorant of dolphin ways, aware only that these were dusky dolphins, one of 33 known species of the family Delphinidae, or true dolphins. After a night of resting near shore to avoid killer whales and sharks, the duskies were on their way to deeper water, scouting for schools of southern anchovy. They were about to participate in what remains one of the most remarkable and well-coordinated examples of cooperative hunting in the mammalian world.

It has taken years to discover how duskies forage, socialize, and care for their young. There is much that we still do not know about these and other dolphins; we have hints and guesses about their social strategies, but we know little with certainty. Pleasantly shining dolphin eyes and smiling faces have long enchanted and beguiled humans; as time goes on, it is likely that we will become ever more impressed by these mammals of the seas.

Mention "dolphin," and most people picture the bottlenose: beaklike snout, bulbous forehead, dark back and whitish belly, and rather large dorsal fin. This is the dolphin made famous by the *Flipper* television series and seen in aquariums worldwide. It is almost cosmopolitan, occurring in all major ocean basins, from the tropics to the 45th parallel of both hemispheres, and into even higher latitudes off Great Britain and New Zealand. It avoids only very cold temperate and polar waters.

But there are many other dolphins, from the nearly five-foot-long Hector's—endemic to New Zealand's waters—to the largest true dolphin, the killer whale. All are rounded, streamlined, with small, paddle-shaped front limbs for steering; a broad, powerful, up-and-down stroking tail for propulsion; and no hind limbs. Different species possess many variations on this basic theme. Male killer whales have rounded front flippers and huge dorsal fins, for example, while right-whale dolphins have no dorsal fins at all. Some dolphins have extenuated jaws; some have blunt heads without a hint of a snout. Some have just a few teeth, others have well over a hundred. Some are a muted dark gray; others are a striking black-and-white—or spotted, striped, or almost pure white. Four species are exclusively riverine, while a fifth is estuarine and coastal; all five have long snouts, many small teeth, and relatively small brains. Then there are six species of porpoises. (While dolphin teeth are peg-shaped or conical, porpoise teeth are spade-shaped; other differences, especially in skull morphology, also help define these two groups.) Finally, two other toothed cetaceans are considered here along with dolphins and porpoises: the beluga whale, or white whale, and the narwhal. Both roam the northern ice. They are the only two species of Monodontidae, a group whose members possess a flat skull—unlike the rounded dolphin skull—and unfused neck vertebrae that allow great head movement relative to the body—unlike the more rigid dolphins.

Some species, such as Hector's dolphins, harbor porpoises, and river dolphins, tend to live in groups of less than a dozen. Others, such as spotted and common dolphins, roam the open seas in throngs of hundreds to thousands. They are reminiscent of ungulate herds grazing the open plains of Africa or primeval North America; all social activities—feeding, detecting and warding off predators, mating, nurturing the young—take place in this large and ever moving society. So it is especially telling that dolphins, like all whales, are derived from an early stock of ungulates. Watch the undulations

BILL CURTSINGER

of a swimming dolphin, the backbone waving up and down as it beats the tailstock, and that action resembles very closely that of a galloping horse or wildebeest. And like wildebeests—or humans—all dolphin species are highly social; while lone individuals do exist, they are not of the norm.

With almost 50 different types of dolphin-like mammals in the world, habitats vary greatly. Some species inhabit the tropics, both for behavioral and physiological reasons; the nearshore river dolphin tucuxi of South and Central America is a good example. It is shaped like a bottlenose dolphin but is only half as long, giving its body a much larger surface-to-volume ratio—making it unlikely to survive the chilly waters of even a temperate ocean in winter. Similarly, other warm-water species, such as spinner, spotted, and

RESEARCH EFFORTS
Helping science answer questions about dolphin life, a bottlenose named Lii learns to butt a sensor suspended 50 feet below a boat. As the device is gradually lowered, Lii follows, last triggering it at 1,550 feet—establishing the diving capability for this species. Near Sarasota, Florida, bottlenose dolphins temporarily get wired for sound with suction-cup microphones in a seagoing corral (opposite, lower) as scientists monitor communications among individuals. Occasional hands-on contact (opposite, upper) keeps the cables from entangling.

DAVID DOUBILET;
FLIP NICKLIN (OPPOSITE BOTH)

A ND LIKE WILDEBEESTS—OR HUMANS—
ALL DOLPHIN SPECIES ARE HIGHLY SOCIAL;
WHILE LONE INDIVIDUALS DO EXIST,
THEY ARE NOT OF THE NORM.

striped dolphins, are larger than tucuxi but thin, with little insulating blubber. At the other extreme are chunky harbor porpoises and beluga whales, fully at home among ice floes and never found in warm waters. In between, we find temperate-water species—white-sided and dusky dolphins, for example—round of body but not rotund. Often they occur antitropically, that is, with identical or closely related varieties in temperate areas of both hemispheres, but not in equatorial waters. We assume that ancestors of these geographically divergent yet morphologically similar forms crossed the Equator during cooler times, perhaps during a wave of glacial advance. There are a few species that have adapted to different climates, often by modifying their sizes. Bottlenose dolphins, for example, average only 8 or 9 feet long in tropical waters, but reach a more heat-conserving size of 11 to 12 feet in seas off Scotland or New Zealand. Only the killer whale is truly cosmopolitan, showing few morphological differences but many behavioral ones throughout many different climatological ranges.

Water depth provides another way to subdivide the dolphin group: Species that frequent inshore waters usually are different from those that cruise nearshore areas—that is, continental shelves and slopes—or those that roam the open ocean. Each group can be tropical (such as the tiny tucuxi and the pale Irrawaddy), or temperate (as is the Hector's dolphin), or cold water (harbor porpoises and belugas). Nearshore species usually travel in bands of dozens to hundreds, while pelagic species occur in groups of hundreds to thousands. Each habitation zone fosters its own feeding habits: While inshore animals usually nose among rocks or vegetation, nearshore animals tend to feed on schooling fish, with open-ocean dolphins preferring lantern fish and squid. In pelagic waters, however, fish and squid generally occur in a food-rich layer that lies just at the edge of light. This layer migrates constantly, sinking hundreds of feet below the surface in daytime and rising to shallower levels at night. Because most pelagic dolphins are not deepwater divers (as are sperm and beaked whales), they are largely night-feeders. A major exception: pilot whales, which can dive beyond 1,600 feet and probably can reach the edge of the food-rich layer at all times.

The clear waters of a tropical sea are as different from a silt-laden estuary as Africa's savannas are from the adjacent jungle highlands. Whatever the habitat, resident animals use their senses and live their lives in different ways. Despite their frozen "smiles," dolphins do not lead carefree lives of blissful ease. They keep constant watch for deepwater sharks and killer whales. They also need food, of course, and risk going hungry when prey species scatter too loosely or for some reason do not rise at night. A dolphin needs all its senses, wits, and social strategies to survive. First, let's consider the senses.

We mammals tend to be adept at smell, taste, touch, sight, and sound. Dogs are better than humans at detecting odors or high-frequency sounds. Cats have excellent eyes, especially well developed for night vision and for movement. Sight is energetically expensive, however, and burrowing animals often exhibit reduced powers of vision, while their senses of smell and touch are particularly acute. Where do dolphins fit in?

They have excellent capabilities of taste, touch, sight, and sound, but no sense of smell. A dolphin's olfactory bulb is a shrunken piece of tissue; its olfactory nerve is similarly shriveled and makes no connection with the brain. It's easy to see how this happened: Although land mammals breathe continuously, the dolphin equivalent of a nose—its blowhole—is closed tightly except for that very brief moment at the surface. But the dolphin's numerous tongue papillae make up in large part for its lack of smell—

Following pages:
A captive dolphin in a large net enclosure off Honduras eyes spiraling fish that blundered near.

NORBERT WU (FOLLOWING PAGES)

OF MAN AND DOLPHIN
In a celebrated fellowship two decades old, visitors to Australia's Shark Bay wade in to feed, photograph, and even pet wild dolphins that willingly venture into the shallows.

because underwater, dissolved chemicals are just as readily tasted as smelled. It is likely that adult dolphins constantly taste each other's urine and feces to gauge sexual readiness and perhaps other aspects of hormonal and emotional states. Male spinner dolphins will nuzzle a female repeatedly, looking for all the world like dogs sniffing each other. In fact, they are *tasting*.

Dolphin skin is so alive with touch receptors that even when one individual approaches another from an angle at which it cannot be seen, it will be detected *before* actual contact. When a dolphin plays with bits of seaweed or human garbage, it can balance an object on its nose, let it slide off, and adroitly catch it with a flipper, dorsal fin, or the forward edge of its flukes. Obviously, it knows where that scrap of flotsam is at any time, and the game, mediated through an exquisite sense of touch, can go on for hours.

Such sensitivity must be very useful in this world where one is always on the move and where friends or foes can come from any direction. Even a dolphin living in clear tropical waters needs to contend not only with the darkness of night, but also with the darkness of depth. It must be reassuring

DAVID DOUBILET; DON KINCAID (OPPOSITE UPPER); FLIP NICKLIN / MINDEN PICTURES (OPPOSITE LOWER)

to be able to detect fellow dolphins to the side or behind, by pressure wave displacement. Although we don't know how sophisticated this tactile sense is, I would not be surprised if it enables a mother to differentiate between her calf and others, or between a juvenile and an adult. Indeed, newborn dolphins often position themselves along the mother's rear flank, and the pressure wave created by the mother's body actually pulls the baby along with little or no energy expenditure of its own.

When it comes to sight, most dolphins are excellently endowed. Their eyes often work in tandem, as ours usually do. But they also use their eyes independently, with one looking forward while the other looks to the side or rear. This ability to switch between coordinated and independent binocular vision is a rarity among mammals. In addition, dolphins can keep one eye open while resting the other, since their brains sleep only one hemisphere at a time. This absence of total sleep is vital. For while sleeping humans can be "dead to the world," sleeping dolphins continue to move through their dangerous environment, and must ascend to breathe every few minutes or so.

In addition, dolphins see as acutely through air as they do through water, a medium more than 800 times as dense. Humans can't—as we know when we open our eyes underwater without a faceplate. But dolphin eyes possess two major physiological adaptations that ours lack: First, they can change shape dramatically, focusing an image on the retina much as a camera focuses by moving the lens nearer to or farther from the film plane. Second, dolphin pupils form a thin slit in bright light, which means greater depth of field, thus sharp vision in air. So it is that trained dolphins and killer whales leap up and unerringly touch their noses to a tossed ball, or gently grasp a fish held by a trainer. Slow-motion photography shows they make subtle in-air corrections during their leaps. In nature, such visual acuity out of water probably helps the animals navigate (by recognizing shorelines), home in on prey (indicated by feeding seabirds), and simply find each other.

Of all senses, hearing is perhaps the dolphin's most remarkable. But then water is an excellent transmitter; in addition, sound waves travel nearly 4.5 times faster than they do in air. Also, sound has few obstructions in the ocean, and it is unhampered by night or turbidity.

Dolphins produce a cacophony of sounds. Many whistle, especially to communicate anger, fright, distress, and other emotions. Young bottlenose dolphins learn what are called "signature whistles"—individually distinctive calls. In studying a particular bottlenose population, Laela Sayigh, of the University of North Carolina, found that some males tended to whistle like their mothers—while females generally did not. Males eventually leave their natal group, but continue to associate periodically with their mothers and other female relatives. Perhaps the whistles help them recognize each other despite long absences; perhaps such recognition helps avoid inbreeding.

GOING ASHORE

Land mammals once, dolphins often return to terra firma, for good or ill. Exact causes of strandings, as with these false killer whales in Florida (upper), continue to baffle scientists—and in fact could vary for different species and populations. Some animals head landward again and again, even after being refloated or towed to sea by well-wishing humans. Headlong chase for fleeing mullet leaves bottlenose dolphins high and nearly dry on a South Carolina shore (above)— but only briefly.

REALM OF DOLPHINS

Dolphins also produce rapid click sequences, called click-trains, that to us sound like squeaky door hinges, rasps, or high-pitched whines. They may be communicative, but it is not clear how they relate to whistles. Certain types of click-trains—usually at frequencies higher than humans can hear—make up an active form of transmission and reception we call echolocation. All animals communicate with their environment. Canids and many ungulates mark important territories with urine or scat, thereby sending an odor-laden message to rivals. Some freshwater fish send and receive electric impulses; fireflies transmit coded bioluminescent flashes in elaborate and visual mating rituals. Bats and dolphins, both at home in three-dimensional environments where prey and predators can be anywhere, echolocate. They send high-frequency click-trains and listen for the returning echoes that bounce off objects within their environment. In this way, they can judge distance, size, shape, even texture, as well as the direction and speed of a potential prey item—or of a predator. Dolphins can also "see" each other sonically. Although we do not as yet know the full story, studies indicate that they can sense differences

among bone, flesh, and air sacs in the body of another animal. Thus they "see" almost in X-ray fashion, and even may be able to tell as much about the health or emotional status of a fellow dolphin as we can determine from the eyes, facial expression, and body language of our colleagues.

Although echolocation has not been proved for all dolphins, it is likely that all have this remarkable capability in some form. But there is a danger to being loquacious at all times, and dolphins that are resting or just traveling through familiar territory may be silent for hours on end. There is little need to advertise oneself to killer whales.

Physically, dolphins and whales are very different from their terrestrial, ungulate ancestors. So, too, are their methods of making sound. That transformation was just as drastic as the loss of hind limbs, the development of a flattened, propulsive tail, and the obliquely positioned diaphragm that can almost totally evacuate air from the lungs. Dolphin whistles and clicks do not originate at the larynx, but at structures known as the monkey lips, which embrace the upper air passages below the blowhole. These passages are paired, and they alternately inflate and deflate, causing air to rush past the monkey lips, which vibrate, producing the clicks. An analogy is the release of air from a balloon; hold the neck of the balloon between your fingers, and by varying the tension you alter the pitch of the sound created

WHALES IN NAME ONLY
Despite the "smile" of a pilot whale (opposite), sea life is no picnic. Scars may stem from bites of cookie-cutter sharks. The bulbous forehead houses the pilot's melon, core organ of its sonar-like echolocation system.

Echolocating clicks help a false killer whale home in on fish (above), while white lips mark six-foot-long pygmy killer whales (upper). All three species are dolphins.

ROBERT PITMAN / EARTHVIEWS (UPPER);
FLIP NICKLIN / MINDEN PICTURES (LOWER);
FLIP NICKLIN (OPPOSITE)

by the vibrating rubber. Dolphins shunt air back and forth without losing any through the blowhole; their system is a closed one. By conserving air, they can remain underwater longer. Ken Norris proposed this mechanism of sound production years ago; despite considerable skepticism from colleagues at the time, recent evidence supports his hypothesis. Dolphin sounds are propagated through the fatty forehead, or melon, out into the environment. The melon actually beams the sound to the front of the animal, its variable intensity apparently enabling it to serve as an "acoustic lens."

But how do dolphins hear? They have no external ear flaps, as do most terrestrial mammals. Again, Norris was the first to postulate a plausible answer. A thin section of lower jaw, he said, could serve as an acoustic window; sound enters the jawbone—which is hollow and filled with a light fat about as dense as seawater—then is channeled to the inner ear. The dolphin's dense lower skull and a complicated collection of air spaces effectively isolate one side of the jaw from the other, helping explain why its hearing is highly directional—a critical requirement for echolocation. Again, despite initial criticism, it now seems that "jaw hearing" is indeed an important part of the dolphin sense of sound. We see dolphins move their heads subtly side-to-side as they home in on a target, apparently comparing sounds that enter opposite sides of the head and distinguishing direction by intensity, arrival time, or by phases of the sound waves. These are remarkable adaptations, especially when one considers that even early odontocetes probably were proficient echolocators, evolving their technique in a relatively short period of time. But then dolphins and whales are remarkable mammals.

As long ago as the 17th century, naturalist and biologist John Ray noticed that dolphins had very large brains for their bodies, with a complexity superficially resembling that of humans. He speculated that they had more than an ordinary wit and capacity. In fact, dolphins *are* intelligent social mammals with very adaptive, quick-learning behavioral capabilities. But how intelligent? One neurosurgeon-turned-dolphinologist predicted that humans and dolphins soon would be conversing with each other, discussing love, death, religion, and other subjects. Obviously, that hasn't happened, and despite some excellent research, we still know very little about how "smart" dolphins really are.

We humans have a hard time defining intelligence. We give tests, assign intelligence quotient (IQ) scores, but we realize that test questions come with the biases of past experiences, cultures, and senses of logic. We are not totally comfortable in stating that one human is more intelligent than another, but we often have a "feeling" for this. So it is with other species. We know that some have larger brains and seem more behaviorally flexible. Spider monkeys and lemurs, for example, are not as intelligent as the great apes. Similarly, harbor porpoises and river dolphins are not as intelligent

FLIP NICKLIN / MINDEN PICTURES

**SCARRED SPY HOPPER
Extensive crisscross scars and a white face mark a Risso's dolphin off Central America. Battered skin is a fact of life among these large, deepwater scrappers, believed to rip at each other in mating rituals with their lower teeth; they have no uppers.**

as bottlenose dolphins or tropical rough-toothed dolphins—whose brain-to-body ratios, by weight, approach those of humans. The latter examples also have large amounts of gray matter, the brain tissue largely responsible for thought. In addition, we know that at least some dolphin species learn tricks quickly, have complicated social relationships in nature, and appear to be highly adaptable and capable of surviving in a dangerous world "with wit." We surmise that they are highly intelligent, but we cannot rank them among more familiar, terrestrial species. Let us hope that further research will shed light on their mental capabilities.

Dolphins in captivity readily associate with humans, generally interact well with trainers, and are more easily trained than many other mammals.

> IN FACT, DOLPHINS *ARE* INTELLIGENT SOCIAL MAMMALS WITH VERY ADAPTIVE, QUICK-LEARNING BEHAVIORAL CAPABILITIES. BUT HOW INTELLIGENT?

They almost seem eager to learn and to please. Their friendliness toward humans stems from their sociability in nature. Within a dolphin school, sociality is immensely important. One obvious advantage to being a social creature is safety; the oceans are full of danger, principally sharks and killer whales. Individual dolphins can see and echolocate, but surprises can come from any direction, and at some time one must rest. A lone dolphin needs to be alert and wary at all times. But in a coordinated society, only one member need detect a potential predator and disseminate an alarm, in order to trigger the appropriate flight or fight response in all the others. For example, dusky dolphins have a screechy sound we call a "killer whale alarm." Whenever it is given, all duskies within hearing range immediately head for shore and hide in the turbulent surf zone, in tidal lagoons, or in other inlets, sometimes for hours. In New Zealand, we found we often could anticipate by several hours the approach of a killer whale pod, simply by watching for the skittish, alarmed movements of their smaller cousins. Sometimes the killer whales were more than ten miles away, leading us to suspect that information had been passed along a grapevine of different groups of dusky dolphins.

Spinner dolphins, so-named because they erupt from the water and rotate up to six times before splashdown, *(Continued on page 159)*

Following pages:
Rough-toothed dolphins streak through Hawaiian waters, perhaps intent on stealing live bait from fishermen's hooks. Though these dolphins get high marks for intelligence, their free-booting ways have given them a reputation as bandits of the deep. They are easily trained, both in captivity and, on occasion, in the open sea, for research. Vertical ridges on the teeth give this largely pelagic, warm-water species its common name. Conical teeth help differentiate dolphins—scattered throughout the world's oceans and rivers—from porpoises, whose teeth are spade-shaped. In general, porpoises also lack the prominent beak or snout of most dolphins, often are smaller, and have much shorter life spans. As with whales, both groups belong to the order Cetacea, and largely accept humans who enter their environment. They also have come under intense human pressures, especially over recent decades. Today they face a spectrum of depredations that range from willful killing to accidental netting, from damming rivers to offshore polluting of the seas with assorted industrial and agricultural chemicals.

ED ROBINSON / TOM STACK AND ASSOCIATES

WOLVES OF THE SEA

Off Argentina, an audience of sea lions watches a killer whale cruise near shore (above). The beach is no guarantee of safety, however, for the surf-patrolling whales (right) routinely launch themselves ashore in quest of tasty sea lion pups (opposite). Once on land, says photographer Jeff Foott, they "work their way back into the water by tail-flopping and waiting for buoyancy from the next wave." Survivors of such attacks learn to recognize the tall dorsal fin and to move farther back from the surf. Killer whales prey also on fish, sea turtles, other dolphins, and even on huge whales—in fact on anything they want.

156 WHALES

BLACK FLAG OF TERROR Warning sign for many a sea denizen, the dorsal fin of the adult male killer whale can measure nearly six feet. The late Michael Bigg, a pioneer in identifying individual killer whales, points to a photograph of the male and the smaller, more curved female dorsal fins (below). A pod of these dolphins cavorts in clear waters off the Solomon Islands,

east of New Guinea (opposite, upper). Family groups bond for life and may include four generations. Two whales rub and roll on pebbly seafloor near Vancouver Island, British Columbia, for no apparent reason other than pure enjoyment (opposite, lower).

can be remarkably silent near shore. In the bays of Hawaii, I have watched an entire school of 40 or 100 animals make only a few echolocation clicks every 15 minutes or so. We assume this is because they are resting after a busy night of feeding on lantern fish and squid in deep oceanic waters; like tired human family members sitting around after a Thanksgiving feast, perhaps they simply don't feel like communicating. Even so, an occasional echolocation click-train serves to scan the environment beyond the capability of sight—and guard against predators. The school also watches for dark silhouettes against the sandy bottom, so that sharks cannot attack unnoticed from the depths. Ken Norris first discovered that spinner dolphins at rest assiduously avoid coral or vegetative areas, presumably because these visual mosaics make detection of predators much more difficult than does uninterrupted sand. Similarly, savanna mammals often avoid brush or forest outcroppings, which can mask a deadly leopard.

Not all dolphins that live close to shore rest in uninterrupted visual habitat. Hector's dolphins off New Zealand and Amazon River dolphins—at times preyed upon by caimans or crocodiles—are remarkably adept at swimming and hiding among rocky outcrops, kelp beds, or submerged roots and branches of a flooded jungle forest. Both dolphin species favor muddy or murky habitats. Their strategy of predator avoidance, it seems, is more like that of dik-diks and other small ungulates that prefer thickets to open plains.

How do dolphins that range far from shore deal with deepwater sharks? Their schools tend to be large, with up to thousands of animals, and although they may attract more attention, they are safer for the individual. For example, in a band of ten, your own chance of being eaten by a highly effective predator is roughly 10 percent. In a group of a hundred, the odds are much less—though not down to one percent, since the group is more visible to a potential predator. Large schools also possess more eyes, ears, and echolocation bursts; they are information processing systems that can nearly totally defeat a predator acting alone.

So it is that open-ocean dolphins often travel in big schools and in even larger, multispecies aggregations. In the tropical Pacific, spinner and spotted dolphins commonly occur together, at times with false killer whales or other toothed cetaceans also mixed in. In the Gulf of Mexico, Atlantic spotted dolphins often join bottlenose dolphins.   *(Continued on page 164)*

KOJI NAKAMURA ; FLIP NICKLIN (OPPOSITE LEFT);
BOB TALBOT (OPPOSITE RIGHT); BIRGITTE WILMS (TOP)

REALM OF DOLPHINS

TOOTHSOME TITANS

For all their ferocity at sea, killer whales seem to adapt well to captivity and often exhibit gentleness with trainers. Human hands and whale teeth come into harmless proximity during feeding time at Sea World in San Diego (above). In a nose-to-nose meeting at an underwater window (opposite), one whale seems as fascinated by children as they are by it. Such tranquil images have been clouded in recent years by injuries inflicted on trainers by performing killer whales. Also, several whales have died in captivity, raising issues such as animal rights. Marine park owners say new male-female mixes among the whales may have sparked aggression toward trainers, and defend whale captivity as a means of public education. The first killer whale born in captivity to live swims above its inverted mother, trailed by another female (following pages). Successes supported aquaria breeding, but the deaths of several males have since severely limited the gene pool for captive killer whales.

FLIP NICKLIN / MINDEN PICTURES (BOTH); SEA WORLD OF FLORIDA (FOLLOWING PAGES)

REALM OF DOLPHINS

Off South America, multispecies aggregations might include dusky dolphins, much larger Risso's dolphins, and pilot whales. We suspect that the different feeding strategies of companion species keep them alert at different times, and that such differences work to the common good. So do their varied physical sizes and echolocation capabilities. The clicks of pilot whales, for example, project much farther than those of dusky dolphins, and the different diving abilities of these species may enable both close and distant warning systems.

Schooling also allows for better detection and capture of prey, easy access to mates, relatively secure and efficient rearing of young, and for other social interactions. Let's discuss these advantages one by one.

Bottlenose dolphins are perfectly able to find and take prey individually, but they also are incredibly adept at coordinated hunting. I have seen them move in single file along the rocky coast of Patagonia, with individual dolphins nosing and poking their snouts among the rocks. When one discovers and chases a sizable fish from its dwelling place, several other dolphins close in from all sides, and—as far as I can tell—share the find. Farther from shore, they often travel abreast of each other, with each dolphin about two to five body lengths from the next, covering as wide a swath of sea as possible. They seek schools of fish, and when they find one, they surround it, at times hitting it from different sides at precisely the same moment. Dolphin maneuvers can be highly coordinated, appearing almost premeditated or at least well practiced, with some individuals pushing the prey toward shore while others—in front, behind, above, and below—prevent their escape. A good game of soccer or polo, with each player knowing his or her position and role, comes to mind.

Once, off Baja California, I watched four bottlenose dolphins traveling about a hundred yards from shore, clearly following a school of several hundred fish perhaps 200 yards ahead. As they neared to within 75 yards—before they could see the fish, but well within echolocation range—the dolphins split into two pairs that moved directly away from each other and then arced in smooth semicircles toward the fish. Remarkably, they arrived from opposite sides at precisely the same instant, causing a welter of confused fish. The dolphins then pushed the alarmed and disoriented school into the shallows and feasted there, where rocks on shore and below, and the dolphins themselves, made escape impossible.

AESTHETIC ATHLETE
A dusky dolphin takes to the air (above), its energetic leaps marking the species as one of the most acrobatic of the cetaceans. Duskies frequent coasts of the Southern Hemisphere, at times traveling in pods that contain a thousand or more members. Icy Antarctic waters draw the hourglass dolphin (left), whose white sides seem to trickle front to back through a narrowed middle. Free-form blush of white names the Atlantic white-sided dolphin (left, lower), still abundant despite being hunted by some nations.

WHALES

At least a dozen other dolphin species hunt cooperatively. So do narwhals, belugas, and—apparently—pilot whales, which plunge nearly half a mile down to feed on fish and squid at the edge of the photic zone, synchronizing their dives among subgroups of a single school. Spotted dolphins in the Gulf of Mexico surround and herd schools of fish at the surface, taking individuals from the periphery while they prevent the schools from scattering or diving. Such contained feeding can go on for hours.

One of my favorite examples of coordinated foraging concerns killer whales. Even more widely distributed than the ubiquitous bottlenose dolphin, killer whales are equally at home in the tropics or near the edge of Antarctic ice, in shallows or in the vast, open ocean. In Puget Sound, they live in resident pods that contain a few to many dozens of individuals, feeding mainly on salmon and other fish. But transient killer whales from as far away as northern Mexico and southern Alaska also appear here occasionally, feeding largely on other marine mammals. In one well-documented instance, about

VANGUARD OF RESEARCH Seemingly pointing the way for killer whale scientist John K. B. Ford of the Vancouver Aquarium and the University of British Columbia, a Pacific white-sided dolphin rides the boat's bow wave.

JIM BORROWMAN; FLIP NICKLIN / MINDEN PICTURES (OPPOSITE UPPER); PAUL ENSOR / HEDGEHOG HOUSE NZ (OPPOSITE MIDDLE); RICHARD SEARS (OPPOSITE LOWER)

REALM OF DOLPHINS

DOLPHINS WITH A TWIST

Aerial artist of its family, the spinner dolphin habitually jumps high out of the water, turning up to six times before splashdown. Acrobatics haven't helped it escape the purse-seine nets of tuna boats, which have cut its numbers in half since 1959. Resting by day, spinners snooze as they slowly cruise Hawaiian waters (above). At night they feed on squid and fish, grasping them in snouts containing up to 248 teeth. Researcher and foundation president Jan Östman-Lind observes and videotapes spinner behavior from an undersea chamber lowered from a boat (below).

WHALES

FLIP NICKLIN / MINDEN PICTURES (ABOVE AND OPPOSITE LOWER); FLIP NICKLIN (OPPOSITE UPPER)

REALM OF DOLPHINS

30 wide-ranging killer whales killed a blue whale, harassing and harrying it as lions might take down a large ungulate on the plains.

Off Argentina and off the Crozet Islands southeast of Africa's Cape of Good Hope, small groups of killer whales specialize in hunting sea lion and elephant seal pups. They repeatedly charge the pebbled shores at high tide, lunging even after their bellies ground, trying to snare young pinnipeds from the surf or the beach itself. Methods vary, but often one will chase a pup along shore, while others station themselves to either side or seaward of the main action, preventing the pup's escape. At times, the scene becomes a teaching situation: The killer whale rushes a specific sea lion or seal again and again, stopping short each time. Then it moves aside, allowing a juvenile

REVEALING THE SLAUGHTER Endangered Species Project biologist Samuel LaBudde, seated before a photograph of a net-drowned dolphin, exposed the killing of dolphins by various fisheries. Working undercover on a tuna boat in 1987, he videotaped the continued netting of dolphins 15 years after the Marine Mammal Protection Act called for their safety. The tapes galvanized activists and stirred many nations to ban tuna caught by nets that also entrap dolphins; in five years, such dolphin deaths dropped by nearly 90 percent.

Duskies are easy to follow while feeding, for they aggregate in groups of a hundred or more, with thousands of seabirds overhead.

killer whale to make its own onshore rush. We can only imagine the precise timing needed to capture another wary and swift marine mammal, and such "lessons" may be critical to acquiring the necessary skills.

Researcher Tiu Similä, of the University of Tromsö in Norway, has found that killer whales there often herd herring into large, ball-like aggregations. The whales swipe their tails against the "ball," apparently to stun and disorient the fish, then leisurely double back and gulp down the confounded prey. Their tail slaps can be sharp and loud, almost like cracks of a rifle.

Similarly, dusky dolphins highly coordinate their foraging activities. Only six or seven feet long, they occur along continental shelves and slopes of the Southern Hemisphere. While they wander into deep canyons, they have never been reported on the high seas and are considered nearshore or semipelagic. I first studied them off Patagonia in the early 1970s, at the invitation of the remarkable marine mammalogist and conservationist Roger Payne. I was a beginning graduate student and was asked to serve as boat driver and diver for Roger and his wife, Katy, who were studying southern right whales. Experienced drivers and divers were easy to find, however, and it was clear that I really was being allowed to tag along because my wife, Melany—also a researcher—was a native Spanish-speaker and could serve as translator—as well as tutor for the Paynes' four pre-teen children. No matter; Melany and I would be able to research dusky dolphins at the same time.

Duskies are easy to find and follow while feeding, for they aggregate in groups of a hundred or more, with thousands of seabirds overhead. But when resting or looking for prey, they split into small bands of a dozen or fewer animals each and can be difficult to track from Patagonia's cliffbound shores. It took a while to unravel their daily routines—sometimes with the aid of radio transmitters attached to individual dolphins. There still is much to learn, but here is an outline of the dusky dolphin day:

At night and in early morning, they rest less than a mile offshore, in water no deeper than 65 feet. They band in groups of 8 to 12 animals, each group as little as half a mile from the next, in a matrix of up to 30 groups. As morning advances, the groups move farther from shore, into 90 or 100 feet of water, and begin zigging and zagging as they forage for fish, all the time staying a half- to a quarter-mile from each other. Apparently, each dolphin band uses click-trains as well as whistle and click communications to

**GREGARIOUS AND FREE
Traveling the open sea in bands of hundreds or more, common dolphins are both fast and widespread. They frolic in the bow waves of whales as well as of boats, and are considered difficult to keep in captivity.**

PETER HOWORTH / MO YUNG PRODUCTIONS (ABOVE); JAMES A. SUGAR & FLIP NICKLIN (OPPOSITE)

REALM OF DOLPHINS

DOLPHIN DRIVE FISHERY

On the beach at Futo on Japan's Izu Peninsula dozens of striped dolphins await processing for human food (left). Dolphin drive fisheries take their name from the procedure by which the cetaceans are rounded up or trapped in enclosures before being slaughtered. Above, a fisherman cuts the carotid artery of a dolphin, causing it to die quickly. In recent years such dolphin drives have happened with less frequency, partly because of bad press and partly because the numbers of dolphins have been depleted. A severed head (below) lies amid offal.

REALM OF DOLPHINS

IN SEARCH OF NARWHALS
A Polar Eskimo returns after his harpoon missed the tusked whale also called "unicorn of the sea." The lone spiral tooth that grows through the upper lip of male narwhals can be a 10-foot-long weapon in mating season. At

times it is used in ritual displays (above). Here, two males cross tusks near the body of a dead female. A narwhal taken by hunters (opposite, upper) is anchored to the ice with its own tooth before being dragged to a butchering site (opposite, lower).

Following pages: Native to the Arctic, narwhals crowd a summertime lead in the ice pack.

detect nearby groups, changing direction whenever they get too close. In this manner, they may cover 30 square miles of sea during the morning hunt. When one dolphin group encounters a school of southern anchovy, it stops; individuals dive down, encircle the fish, and herd them up to the surface. Up to this point, their actions are not particularly amazing, for many animals coordinate to corral schooling prey. Predatory jacks, for example, herd silversides in coordinated fashion. But duskies do more.

As soon as the fish are herded to the surface, nearby dolphin groups race in, drawn apparently by the leaps and splashes of dolphins trying to contain the prey. Perhaps the leaping is a communal call, something like, "Come help us herd!"

Aggregating is very important to duskies, because a band of ten cannot effectively herd, contain, and feed on a fish school. Feeding dolphins disrupt the fish, and nonfeeders are needed to keep them tightly balled against the surface. Thus, the arrival of other dolphin bands helps perpetuate the activity; new arrivals help herd, then take turns at feeding. Simultaneously, gulls, terns, cormorants, shearwaters, petrels, and albatrosses also move in, creating a blizzard of birds overhead. It is all highly visual, alerting even more distant dolphins. We have witnessed feeding sessions that involved all 300 or so local dolphins and went on for two to three hours.

In addition, we found, arriving dolphins help find other fish schools in the area and bring them to the surface. Biologists call this a fission-fusion society, because groupings alternately coalesce and split up. The coordinated nature of the hunt and the fact that no one dolphin appears to feed until the prey have been secured are reminiscent of the cooperative hunting strategies of wolves and other social terrestrial mammals.

As feeding progresses, duskies caress and even mate with other members of the larger group. Mating occurs even when animals are not in estrus, and we suspect that the high incidence of sex and social activity after feeding is vital to the society's structure. Animals who work side-by-side may gauge each other's capabilities, and then renew or strengthen social bonds, possibly social hierarchies as well. This, I stress, is my own speculation. But social greeting ceremonies and "parties" are well known for primate societies; a dolphin party following a feeding—when duskies have just completed an essential requisite of life—may be especially important. "We got together as a large school; we worked well together; we now need to reaffirm social ties so that we will work well together again"—I can almost hear them saying it, but I also may be wide of the mark.

FLIP NICKLIN / MINDEN PICTURES (ABOVE AND OPPOSITE LEFT); IVARS SILIS (OPPOSITE RIGHT); FLIP NICKLIN (FOLLOWING PAGES)

REALM OF DOLPHINS

WHALE MEAT SUBSTITUTE
A Dall's porpoise comes ashore from a fishing boat in northern Honshū. Japan's annual take of these largest of all porpoises increased sharply in the late 1980s, following a near-total ban on the killing of great whales. Some 40,000 were deliberately harvested in 1988, while others were taken as bycatch in drift and salmon nets. By 1994, controls instituted by the Japanese government helped reduce the yearly take to 11,403.

The degree of cooperation that appears to be the norm with dusky and some other dolphin societies brings up the question, who benefits? I suspect that individuals who cooperate get more food than those who do not. Cheaters in this society—for example those who do not practice temporary restraint during herding—might well be ostracized in some way. Cooperation could be kin-based, with mothers and daughters helping each other and thus benefiting their mutual genes. But to do more than speculate, we must have much better data—information on long-term bonds, detailed information on who does what, for, and with whom.

All through spring, summer, and fall in southern Argentina, dusky dolphins display their remarkable fission-fusion society. Such behavior hinges on the presence of tightly schooled fish. But in the austral winter, when southern anchovies grow less abundant or even absent, most duskies migrate north. The few that remain totally change their foraging strategy and group composition. They appear to feed in bands of 8 to 12 individuals on nearshore and shallow-water bottom fish, staying close to land and hardly ever coalescing into larger groups. They forage mostly at night and rest during the day, a complete reversal of their activity pattern for the rest of the year. No fission-fusion society, no intergroup coordination, no parties. No need to stray into deeper waters where potential danger threatens.

Half a world away from Patagonia's shallow shores, off New Zealand's South Island, dusky dolphins display very different lifestyles, for the habitat is also very different. New Zealand's sharper drop-offs bring deep water very close to land; duskies feed in those nearshore abysses, not on schooling fish but on deepwater lantern fish and squid, which rise nightly toward the surface and sink during the day. As a result, dolphins here generally feed at night, then rest and socialize during the day in shallow waters. There is no need to spread out over a large area to find food, since their kitchen lies predictably at the drop-off zone. Nor is there a daytime advantage to splitting up, so New Zealand duskies tend to stay in the larger-group envelope. While mothers with newborn calves may draw away from the herd, there is no true fission-fusion society related to finding and securing food, as in Argentina.

Hawaiian spinner dolphins live a lifestyle that falls somewhere between the two dusky populations just noted. Studied by Ken Norris and others since the early 1970s, such dolphins exhibit fission-fusion society—like Argentine duskies—but also feed at night on deepwater organisms—much like New Zealand's duskies. They form large, nocturnal groups of several hundred animals, surfacing and diving in rough synchrony as they alternate their need to breathe and to feed. But as the sun rises and prey sink out of reach, spinners head for shore to avoid predators and rest in shallow, clear waters. The available bays are small, however, so the dolphin envelope splits into smaller groups, the extent of fission and fusion related to the size limitations of the habitat rather than to the efficiency of securing food.

Another vital part of the dolphin social system consists of sexual strategy: Who gets to mate with whom? Within or outside a given group? We have good knowledge of bottlenose dolphins, thanks largely to long-term studies by Randall Wells of the Chicago Zoological Society and his colleagues in the Sarasota-Bradenton area of western Florida. Randall has been observing the same resident bottlenose dolphins since 1970, recognizing individuals by dorsal fin markings and periodically capturing them to obtain age, health, and other data. Some are more than 50 years old. Behavioral and genetic data indicate that this society is a "multimate" one; each adult female and male are likely to copulate with more than one of the opposite sex. Since a female in this population has only one young every three to six years, it is to

DYING BREED?
One of the last of its kind, this vaquita held by a Mexican fisherman (right) died in nets meant for sharks. Also known as the Gulf of California harbor porpoise because of its limited habitat, this small cetacean, discovered by science only in 1958, now numbers less than 200 animals. A happier fate awaits a harbor porpoise (below) found alive in a Bay of Fundy herring trap. Canadian biologist Andrew Read returns it to the wild.

FLIP NICKLIN (ABOVE AND OPPOSITE); FLIP NICKLIN / MINDEN PICTURES (TOP)

her benefit to seek the most robust, genetically fit males as partners. Indeed, genetic data often show that youngsters of the same mother have different fathers, and sometimes these fathers are from outside the community.

The bottlenose dolphins studied by Wells display a fission-fusion society. Although they rarely get together into a superschool as duskies do, school memberships can fluctuate greatly. It is very likely that all of the hundred or so individuals in this study area know each other well. It also is probable that the openness of this society reflects individual preferences and perhaps bonds that increase the efficiency of particular social interactions. The society is matriarchal. Female young tend to stay in the home range of their mothers and grandmothers, so they interact more frequently than male

FINLESS WONDERS
Slim profiles and lack of dorsal fins give northern right-whale dolphins a svelte look as they make low-angle leaps in the northern Pacific (upper). Their southern counterparts sport white faces (above). Both species were named for their much larger but similarly shaped cousins. As if blanched by the warm Asian waters they prefer, finless porpoises (opposite, lower) resemble small belugas. They often travel with the hump-backed dolphin (opposite, upper), whose pointed snout contrasts with the blunt beaks of the porpoises.

But it seems certain that, like other social mammals inhabiting a harsh world, dolphins rely on competition and aggressiveness to survive.

offspring do. Males spend several early years with their mothers but as adults often form strong pair bonds with other males and range over wider areas, visiting other groups and other females.

Mammal mothers always know who their offspring are, at least while they are nursing them. But males in a multimate society have no assurance that a particular youngster is their own. It is possible that brothers can recognize each other, perhaps by similarities in whistles and by knowing who their mother is. Thus we would expect brothers (who, since they are likely to have different fathers, are actually *half*-brothers) to more often assist each other than to assist non-kin, but we have no information on this point.

In western Australia, near the village of Monkey Mia on Shark Bay, most dolphins remain offshore. But about a dozen of them habitually swim into the shallows to be fed and petted by humans. They've been doing it for at least the past 20 years, providing visitors with unusual experiences and biologists with excellent opportunities. Richard Connor and Rachel Smolker, of the Univeristy of Michigan (Ann Arbor), began a study of bottlenose dolphins here in the early 1980s. They observed fission-fusion behavior, as well as schooling along matriarchal lines—traits shared by Florida bottlenose dolphins. They also discovered something else: At Monkey Mia, male dolphins form coalitions to kidnap females, often for hours and sometimes for days. This may be a mating strategy for males that are not chosen by females. At any rate, their coalitions aggressively sequester single females and actively defend them from other males. Similar male cooperation has been described for sea lions, as well as for several primate species. We do not know whether such coalitions have a dominance order, or if they are kin-based. But it seems certain that, like other social mammals inhabiting a harsh world, dolphins rely on competition and aggressiveness to survive. Connor and Smolker also discovered female-based alliances, which may ward off unwanted males and also may be useful in foraging and in protecting the females from sharks.

Following pages: Shadowing her subjects through clear Bahamian waters, researcher Denise Herzing of The Wild Dolphin Project follows free-swimming Atlantic spotted dolphins for hours at a time, recording their behavior with video and sound equipment.

Southern dusky dolphins, spinner dolphins, and most small dolphins of the open ocean associate in much larger groups than do nearshore bottlenose dolphins. But within such pods—even those that never split up in fission-fusion fashion—separate subgroups exist, defined apparently by maternal associations and by age groups. They appear remarkably like the smaller schools of bottlenose dolphins that travel out of sight of each other. Also, they may well be multimate, with the closest long-term bonds occurring among mothers and female offspring.

One characteristic common to most dolphin species concerns the testes: They are enormous, relative to body size, and they produce large quantities of sperm. Such qualities are seen in both multimate and polygynous societies, where one male mates repeatedly with many different females. Since only one sperm can inseminate an egg—and since, in dolphins, a successful fertilization will be the only one for that particular female for at least two years—competition among males is to be expected. In many dolphin species it occurs essentially at the sperm level. Thus it behooves males to copulate as often as possible with as much sperm as possible, in order to "flood out" contributions from other males and propagate their own genes into the next generation. The formation of male coalitions to sequester females could be an example of competition being muted at the behavioral level in favor of the physiological level.

KENNETH C. BALCOMB / EARTHVIEWS; STEVE DAWSON / HEDGEHOG HOUSE NZ (TOP) (BOTH PHOTOGRAPHS ON THIS PAGE SHOW ANIMALS IN CAPTIVITY); ROBERT PITMAN / EARTHVIEWS (OPPOSITE UPPER); DENNIS BUURMAN / HEDGEHOG HOUSE NZ (OPPOSITE LOWER); FLIP NICKLIN (FOLLOWING PAGES)

Sexual dimorphism, in which males and females differ greatly in physical appearance, often indicates the prevalent mating strategy for that species. In highly polygynous animals—such as elephant seals, sea lions,

REALM OF DOLPHINS

and fur seals—males are much larger than females. Among elk and lions, huge antlers and manes advertise the males, which display toward each other and battle for dominance, while females often exercise considerable choice in mate selection. We see strong sexual dimorphism in sperm whales, which are polygynous, and in beaked whales. Most cetaceans, however, show only muted dimorphism; it is quite difficult to tell males from females among com-

mon, spotted, bottlenose, or Hector's dolphins, for example. Physical similarity between the sexes argues against polygyny. Social organization and observed mating behavior indicate that the animals are not monogamous either, but engage in a multimate strategy.

Of the dolphin types, strong sexual dimorphism marks narwhals, pilot whales, killer whales, and one population of spinner dolphins. Narwhal males grow a prodigiously long canine, advertising their maleness and age for all to see. They also travel together, and in some areas have entirely different migratory routes from females and young. Like medieval knights, they sometimes spar with their tusks; we assume they do so to establish dominance and secure access to females. Pilot whale males are larger than females and develop a particularly thick and wide dorsal fin that droops at the top as they get older. In this matriarchal society, females remain able to nurse even after menopause. Relatives may share nursing duties. Prolonged nursing occurs on occasion and may be part of the tight bonding that is known for this species. Pilot whale society is either multimate or polygynous, and because of the sexual dimorphism, I suspect the latter.

DAN SAMMIS; FLIP NICKLIN (UPPER); JAMES D. WATT (OPPOSITE)

Male killer whales are much larger than females, with huge dorsal fins. A 30-foot male can have a dorsal fin fully 6 feet high, certainly a splendid and easily recognized secondary sex characteristic. Killer whales that feed primarily on salmon in the Puget Sound–Vancouver area live in remarkably stable pods; males do not leave their mothers, and all offspring stay together for life. Theirs is a closed society, highly unusual among mammals. A pod might consist of grandmother, mother, several aunts, daughters, and sons. Only the fathers are absent, as males apparently mate outside of their natal group during periodic get-togethers known as "superpods." We assume that superpods afford males the opportunity to impress each other and females with their bodily bulk and their dorsal fin size. Killer whales are either polygynous or multimate, but once again, we do not know for sure.

LIFE IN THE WILD
Acclimated to Denise Herzing's presence, wild Atlantic spotted dolphins carry on as usual. One male inverts to mate with a female (opposite, upper), while others stir up sand in search of small fish hiding there (opposite, lower). Other divers accompanying Denise gain similar acceptance from the dolphins. Recalls Flip Nicklin, "They actually slowed down so we could keep up. One swam within arm's length and posed for me." These highly social dolphins continue to cluster even while surfing a boat's bow wave (left). Juveniles are lighter hued than adults, with fewer freckles—making them easily confused with bottlenose dolphins. The species is considered common in the western North Atlantic and the Gulf of Mexico.

183

Just as social structures adapt to different habitats, so sexual systems vary somewhat among different populations of the same species. A multimate system among Florida bottlenose dolphins does not preclude polygyny— or perhaps even monogamy—elsewhere. Much more work needs to be done, and certainly there will be surprises.

As successful as any cetacean sexual strategy may be, it obviously could neither foresee nor compensate for the impact of humans. Centuries of whaling ravaged the world's blue, fin, sei, right, humpback, bowhead, and gray whales, among others. Fortunately, these species became economically extinct before they did so biologically. All but northern right whales are doing better now, after concerted pressures led to international protection.

Threats...are many: Bycatch of different fisheries, direct exploitation for bait and human consumption, loss and degradation of habitat.

UNCERTAIN FUTURE
Nearly ten feet long, the boto, or Amazon River dolphin, ranks as the world's largest freshwater dolphin (upper). Its unique color lends it yet another name: pink dolphin. Though still widespread throughout Amazonia and numerous in some areas, it faces many threats, including dams, pollution, outboard motors, and fishnets. Rescued from the Orinoco, two botos (above) show the ridged back of their species. It lacks the true dorsal fin of their look-alike, the seagoing tucuxi (below).

But the situation remains bleak for several entire species of small toothed cetaceans, as well as for populations of many other species.

Today's most critically endangered cetaceans are the vaquita, baiji, and bhulan. All three inhabit relatively restricted ranges, in nearshore or inshore waters heavily used by humans. The vaquita, endemic to the northern Gulf of California, today numbers less than 200. It suffers from accidental drownings in fishnets, from human overfishing of its prey species, and from habitat degradation that ranges from damming of the Colorado River to relentless bottom-scouring by shrimpers. The baiji, or Yangtze River dolphin of central China, is plagued by similar problems. Entanglement in nets and a type of fishery called rolling-hook fishing kill many directly, while overfishing of prey, damming of tributaries, and heavy industrial and agricultural pollution of the mighty Yangtze all impair the baiji's favored habitat. Much the same story holds true also for the little bhulan, or Indus River dolphin, which has been subjected to accidental netting, pollution, and numerous weirs and dams that fragment the river network.

In addition, specific populations of many other delphinid species face critical dangers. Off Peru and Chile, for example, fishermen take dusky, Commerson's, and black dolphins for human consumption as well as for baiting their crab pots. Nearshore fishing nets accidentally kill harbor porpoises in the western North Atlantic as well as in the Black Sea. They also snag finless porpoises off Japan, Indochina, and Thailand. Southeast Asia's Irrawaddy dolphins suffer greatly from habitat degradation, while humpbacked dolphins of the Indian Ocean and western Pacific are especially threatened near such human-impacted areas as Macau and Hong Kong. Even the bottlenose dolphin is not immune, for periodic die-offs afflict its North Atlantic and Gulf of Mexico populations. The probable cause is toxin accumulation from these heavily developed, nearshore habitats.

Threats to toothed cetaceans are many: Bycatch of different fisheries, direct exploitation for bait and human consumption, loss and degradation of habitat. The latter includes overfishing, habitat alteration from dams or other structures, ever increasing commercial and recreational use of bays and estuaries, and pollution by factory effluents and agricultural runoff. The last

TROUBLED WATERS
Endemic to the Yangtze River, China's baiji now barely survives. It may number fewer than 300. Officially protected, it suffers from bycatch, boat traffic, and pollution.

BERND WÜRSIG (PHOTOGRAPH SHOWS ANIMAL IN CAPTIVITY); FERNANDO TRUJILLO (OPPOSITE UPPER); GREGORY OCHOCKI (OPPOSITE MIDDLE); FLIP NICKLIN / MINDEN PICTURES (OPPOSITE LOWER)

threat—toxins flowing into the environment—is probably the hardest to control and therefore the most insidious. We know that massive, recent die-offs of striped dolphins in the western Mediterranean and bottlenose dolphins in the western North Atlantic were due largely to invasions of an often fatal viral infection classed as morbillivirus. Affected dolphins showed high toxin loads in their bodies, and we assume from studies of terrestrial mammals that such poisons impair the body's normal immune response, which could explain the catastrophic viral infections. Dolphins are at or near the top of the food chain, feeding generally on fish that have themselves fed on smaller fish and invertebrates. Thus they accumulate toxins in high concentrations, usually in their body fat, or blubber. When they eat less than usual due to weather or other factors, stored fats are metabolized, releasing the stored toxins all at once into their systems, poisoning or even killing them. Such deaths by unseen toxins are difficult to trace and harder to control.

STEVE DAWSON

At least one firm connection has been shown, however: Beluga whales of the degraded St. Lawrence River are in desperate trouble. Daniel Martineau of the University of Montreal, Pierre Béland of the St. Lawrence National Institute of Ecotoxicology, and their coworkers have shown that about 500 belugas survive in the St. Lawrence, from a population that once stood at 5,000 or more. The dead that wash ashore show high levels of heavy metals, PCBs, and DDE (a breakdown product of DDT) in their bodies. They also exhibit various growths, cancers, apparent genetic deformities, and other pathological problems in much higher concentrations than do beluga populations of pristine areas. These researchers hypothesize that aluminum factories, paper mills, and other industries, as well as agricultural runoff from both the northern U.S. and southern Canada, contribute to this lethal toxic brew. French-Canadian researcher Nathalie Patenaude, currently with the University of Auckland in New Zealand, and her colleagues found a higher genetic relatedness in St. Lawrence beluga whales than in another population—one indication that they may be suffering the added ills of inbreeding.

How can we expect developing or protein-poor nations to stop hunting whales and polluting habitats, when this beluga population, shared by two of the earth's most environmentally aware nations, faces extinction? Only rapid increases in awareness and environmental action, by many nations, can help avoid catastrophe for the world's whales and their ecosystems.

Yet some encouraging signs exist. International attention has helped outlaw the purposeful taking of dolphins in the Philippines, Peru, and Chile. While some killing continues clandestinely, it is less than the wholesale slaughter of even a few years ago. The Hector's dolphin of New Zealand, one of the smallest true dolphins, has been in sharp decline in some areas, due to entanglements in gill nets set by both commercial and by noncommercial fishermen. But now, the establishment of a dolphin sanctuary near the relatively populous Banks Peninsula of South Island augurs a brighter future for this species. New Zealand researchers Steve Dawson and Elisabeth Slooten, both of Otago University, brought the Hector's plight to international attention and tirelessly campaigned for the sanctuary's creation. Similarly, William Perrin, Stephen Leatherwood, and Randall Reeves—past and present officers of the Cetacean Specialist Group of the International Union for the Conservation of Nature and Natural Resources (IUCN)—have brought the plight of dozens of cetacean species to the attention of researchers, conservationists, and governments, and have initiated strategies for 13 especially hard-hit species and dozens of endangered populations worldwide.

Research, of course, is vital to discovering and detailing population sizes, trends, and specific threats. Armed with knowledge, we can present alternative fishing techniques and alternatives to poisoning or otherwise degrading the environment. For the vaquita, baiji, and bhulan, these efforts

UNDERSEA GALLOWS

A gill net off the South Island of New Zealand claims a Hector's dolphin, which drowned when it could not reach the surface. Designed to trap fish of a size just larger than its mesh, gill nets also kill other marine life, indiscriminately. Drift nets—made of fine, nearly invisible monofilament and running up to 40 miles long—have proved even more destructive. Suspended far below floats, such "curtains of death" drift over open seas, entangling whales, dolphins, seabirds, seals, sharks, and unsellable fish, along with targeted catches. Lost in storms or cut loose after being damaged, they continue killing for weeks, until the weight of wasted bodies drags them to the bottom. The United Nations' resolution to prohibit large-scale drift nets took effect in 1992, and major fishing nations such as Japan and South Korea now follow the ban, after initially opposing it. Yet Italian and French boats still cast miles-long nets in the Mediterranean. In New Zealand, new fishing regulations limit the setting of nets somewhat, but fisheries' bycatch of dolphins continues worldwide.

UNDER SIEGE

Beluga whale swollen with a full-term fetus and bloated by death gets a tow up the St. Lawrence River to Tadoussac, Quebec, for necropsy. Pollution is suspected. Although most of the world's estimated 100,000 belugas, or white whales, live in Arctic waters, glacial retreat at the end of the last ice age trapped a remnant population in the St. Lawrence. The perhaps 500 living here now are besieged by pollution. When tested, their bodies reveal a toxic brew of chemical effluent from aluminum smelters and other riverside industries. The fact that these coldwater animals inhabit an increasingly temperate area may add to fatalities. Noise pollution in the busy river also may badger the whales, which communicate in a rich acoustical "language" of clicks, whistles, warbles, and trills. Early mariners dubbed them sea canaries for the sounds that could be heard through wooden hulls. A modern tourist ship pauses so passengers can observe the passage of three belugas (above).

REALM OF DOLPHINS

may be a case of too little, too late. Even so, Zhou Kaiya, of Nanjing's Normal University, and a cadre of cetacean researchers at the Wuhan Institute of Hydrobiology are teaming with Western scientists to catch the few remaining baiji and transport them to controlled byways of the Yangtze, where they may yet survive and procreate in captivity.

Our best hope for conserving cetaceans may be our almost natural love for them. Dolphins were revered by the ancient Greeks and Romans, and stories of dolphins befriending humans abound. Such "friendships" can become ever more prevalent when we humans see nature not as merely something ripe for conquest, but as a part of ourselves. Dolphins and people—as far apart as Mauritania and southern Brazil—have for generations

> OUR BEST HOPE FOR CONSERVING CETACEANS MAY BE OUR ALMOST NATURAL LOVE FOR THEM.... STORIES OF DOLPHINS BEFRIENDING HUMANS ABOUND.

participated in cooperative fish hunts: The dolphins drive the finned prey toward the fishermen's waiting nets, while the humans toss back a portion of their take to the dolphins. At many other sites, the blossoming of tourism over the past 20 years has focused on whales and dolphins as objects of wonder just offshore, not mere receptacles of oil and flesh.

Off New Zealand, where Melany and I have studied dusky dolphins since 1984, swim-with-dolphin tours now occur in about ten different areas, featuring four different species. The little town of Kaikoura on the east side of New Zealand's South Island was a sleepy fishing and sheep farming village when we first arrived. Once it had been a center of whaling for humpback and sperm whales, then it became the core of a lucrative fishing, lobstering, and oystering industry. As it exhausted those resources, the town began turning away from the sea—until someone started a whale-and-dolphin tourism enterprise in 1988. It is now again a boomtown, with people who love nature—and marine mammals especially—coming from all over the world to see and be with sperm whales, as well as with Hector's, dusky, and common dolphins. Just about every villager is proud of this new association, which benefits not only residents but also thousands of other people. Local marine life has benefited too, as Kaikoura has moved from the consumptive

SITTING HIGH AND TOO DRY
A fast ebb tide strands a beluga whale off Somerset Island, northern Canada, while sunburn takes its toll (above). Yearly visits to rub off dead winter skin in gravelly shallows can leave these 3,000-pounders land-bound—and vulnerable to predators—for hours. This animal swam off, but another (right) succumbed to a polar bear. Elsewhere on Somerset, bank-to-bank belugas crowd an inlet (opposite) to molt; researchers seek clues to their movements by pinning a satellite transmitter to a 15-footer.

and potentially destructive pursuits of whaling and fishing to the far more sustainable industry of tourism.

Even in Japan, where whaling has been practiced for several centuries, whale-watching and swim-with-dolphin activities are on the rise. A developing tourism effort in Indonesia promises to redirect some of the fishing economy in areas inhabited by Irrawaddy dolphins. Certainly, tourism is not the only answer, and it must be strictly regulated or we risk the chance of too many humans and boats degrading the very environment and species that need protection. Those who come to celebrate natural beauty are ever increasing, and nature always has limits. Overall, however, tourism is much more sustainable economically—and much more satisfying—than are those human enterprises that cause nature's demise, often in the name of progress.

Again and again, as I watch from shore or a small boat while dusky dolphins socialize and leap by day, then go off to feed on anchovy—or on deepwater fish and squid—I come full circle to reflect on my first experience with these wonderful fellow mammals. Twenty-five years ago, very few

REALM OF DOLPHINS

ALL EYES ON THE VISITOR Belugas in Lancaster Sound in Canada's Northwest Territories flip upside-down and keep on swimming, to better examine the photographer watching them from the surface. Their position may also help them define the stranger by focusing sonar-like signals from their bulging melons. The mobility of beluga necks and their musculature give these animals very expressive faces. "They also show more curiosity than any other whales I've ever encountered," says lensman Flip Nicklin. Long hunted for oil, muktuk, and meat, belugas now are taken legally only by subsistence whalers. When not massing in bays and river inlets in summer, the white whales live in small groups of 10 or 20 throughout the Arctic, using echolocation to maneuver under and around the ice.

***Following pages:* Like shards split from the surrounding floes, a pale beluga cow and her grayish calf move through an ice-choked strait in polar Canada.**

FLIP NICKLIN
(OPPOSITE AND FOLLOWING PAGES)

people gave themselves the chance to see whales and dolphins in nature. Hardly anyone ducked a head underwater to experience them in their own milieu. Now hundreds to thousands do so every day, perhaps tens of thousands in a single year. Every one of them, I hope, comes away with the same exhilaration, the sense of wonder and awe which I first felt back in 1971 and continue to experience even now, whenever I see dolphins. They do not much resemble us terrestrial beings anatomically, what with their lack of legs, their propulsive paddles, and their sleek, fat-encased bodies. But when we look into their eyes and observe their actions, we recognize them as intelligent, social mammals. We know they care long and well for their young. We witness their excellent cooperation as they herd and contain their

> THEY DO NOT MUCH RESEMBLE US.... BUT WHEN WE LOOK INTO THEIR EYES AND OBSERVE THEIR ACTIONS, WE RECOGNIZE THEM AS INTELLIGENT, SOCIAL MAMMALS.

prey, and we watch them communicate in ways so sophisticated that we've only just begun to comprehend. And we come to the conclusion that, despite their many obvious differences, they are one of us.

We humans have played the lords of nature for a long time now. We are beginning to realize that although we may be wonderful examples of evolutionary success, all parts of the natural world—from the grubs and worms and beetles that till the soil to the forests that nourish our atmosphere—also have passed evolution's numerous tests, and are intricately related to us. As we have ruled earth's varied domains, so we have managed to destroy parts of them here and there. I do not think we should respect dolphins and whales more than other representatives of the natural world, more than coral reefs or plankton, for example, or the shorelines or oceanic currents that have helped whales evolve to their present, magnificent states. Still, we can look at whales and realize that, without these creatures and their natural realms, we ourselves would be much less.

My hope is that, some day soon, we will see them as examples, as emissaries if you will, of another group of social beings living in overall harmony with their surroundings—and that perhaps from them we can learn to do as well in our world as they have in theirs.

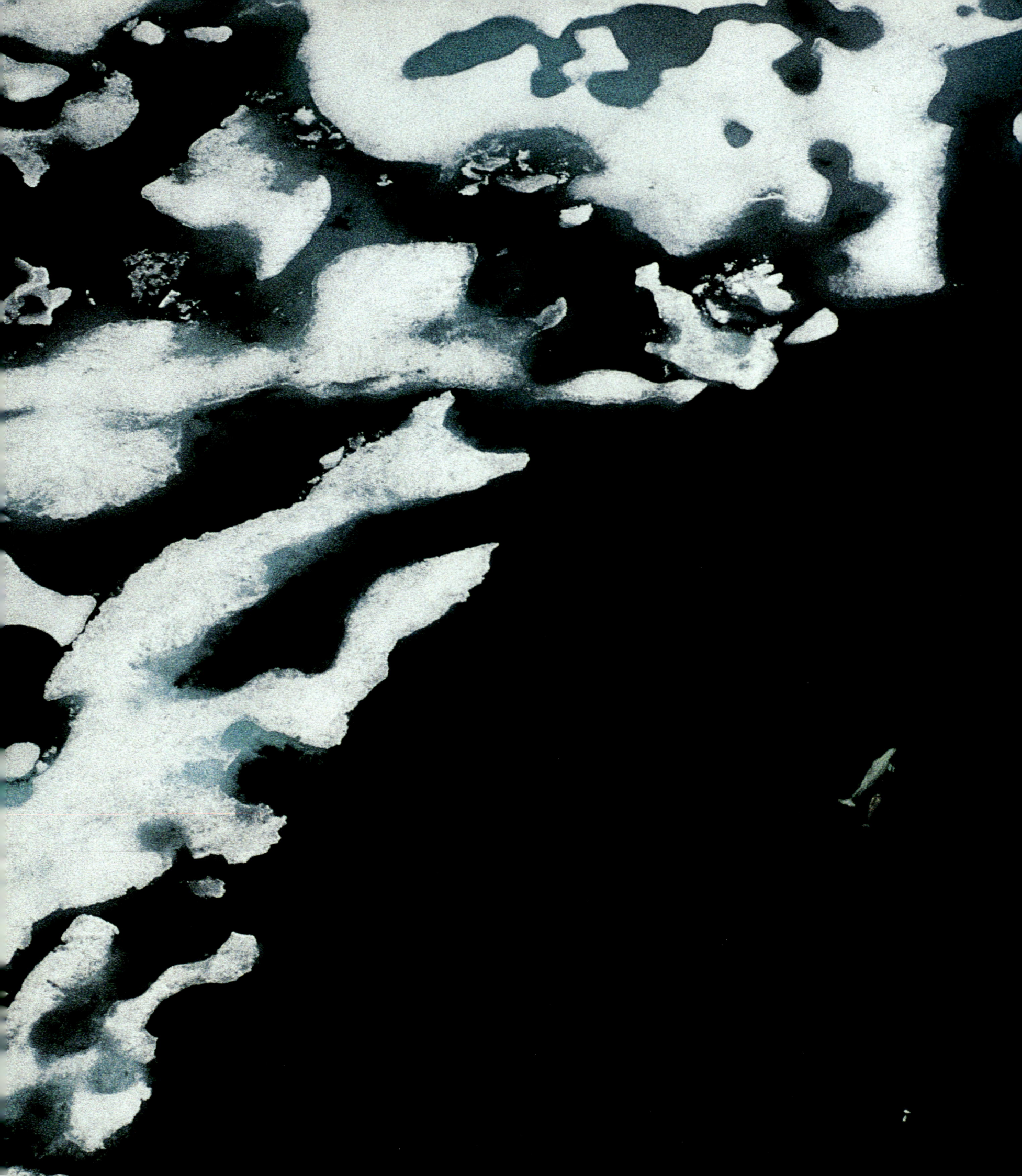

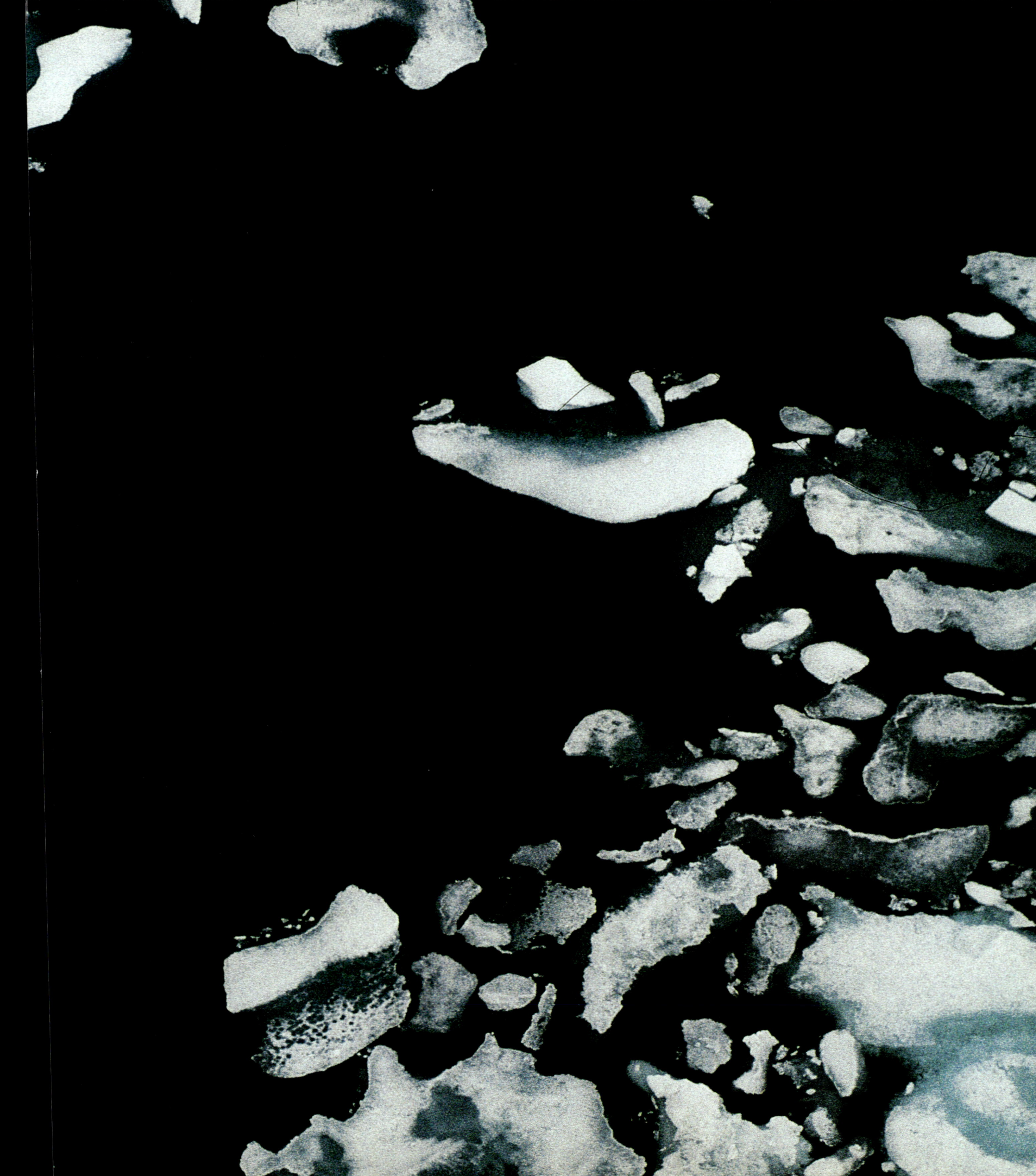

DOLPHINS PORPOISES

CHAPTER FOUR

They are our kindred spirits in the sea, mammals supremely adapted to a life underwater. Dolphins and porpoises share qualities with us that many land animals do not. They accept us when we enter their world. They possess brains with complexities similar to our own, and can follow complicated directions. We have much to learn about the sea—the most extensive environment on our planet and one that we are altering—as well as its creatures. Dolphins and porpoises offer a bridge toward understanding that alien realm beneath the waves, and ongoing research continues to unveil amazing information about them:

- DOLPHINS AND PORPOISES can rest one side of their brains at a time, allowing the other side to remain vigilant for danger.

- THEY CREATE SOUNDS in a closed system that leaks no air, and they beam those signals outward from organs in their heads known as melons.

- THEIR ECHOLOCATING SYSTEMS allow them to "see" undersea creatures in X-ray fashion, determining body make-up and—possibly—emotional states.

- MALE DOLPHINS LEFT OUT of breeding groups may form coalitions that kidnap females for mating; female groups may ward off unwanted males.

- DOLPHINS APPEAR CAPABLE of long-distance communication by relaying messages among different groups. For example, pods of dusky dolphins have been known to show alarm when approaching killer whales are still miles away.

Playful killer whales breach in Johnstone Strait near Vancouver. Once seen simply as bloodthirsty, they are increasingly viewed as intelligent and highly social.

REALM OF DOLPHINS

FAMILIES AND SPECIES

Family Platanistidae

Susu (Ganges River dolphin)
Bhulan (Indus River dolphin)

Family Pontoporiidae

Franciscana (La Plata dolphin)
Baiji (Yangtze River dolphin)

Family Iniidae

Boto (Amazon River dolphin)

Family Delphinidae

Tucuxi
Indo-Pacific hump-backed dolphin
Atlantic hump-backed dolphin
Rough-toothed dolphin
Bottlenose dolphin
Atlantic white-sided dolphin
White-beaked dolphin
Pacific white-sided dolphin
Dusky dolphin
Hourglass dolphin
Peale's dolphin
Fraser's dolphin
Commerson's dolphin
Hector's dolphin
Heaviside's dolphin
Black (Chilean) dolphin
Northern right-whale dolphin
Southern right-whale dolphin
Short-beaked common dolphin
Long-beaked common dolphin
Spinner dolphin
Clymene dolphin
Pantropical spotted dolphin
Atlantic spotted dolphin
Striped dolphin
Risso's dolphin
Irrawaddy dolphin
Melon-headed whale
Pygmy killer whale
False killer whale
Killer whale
Short-finned pilot whale
Long-finned pilot whale

Family Monodontidae

Narwhal
Beluga

Family Phocoenidae

Harbor porpoise
Burmeister's porpoise
Vaquita
Finless porpoise
Spectacled porpoise
Dall's porpoise

Spotted dolphins frolic alongside a shrimp boat off Costa Rica, banking on a handout of bycatch tossed overboard.

BILL CURTSINGER

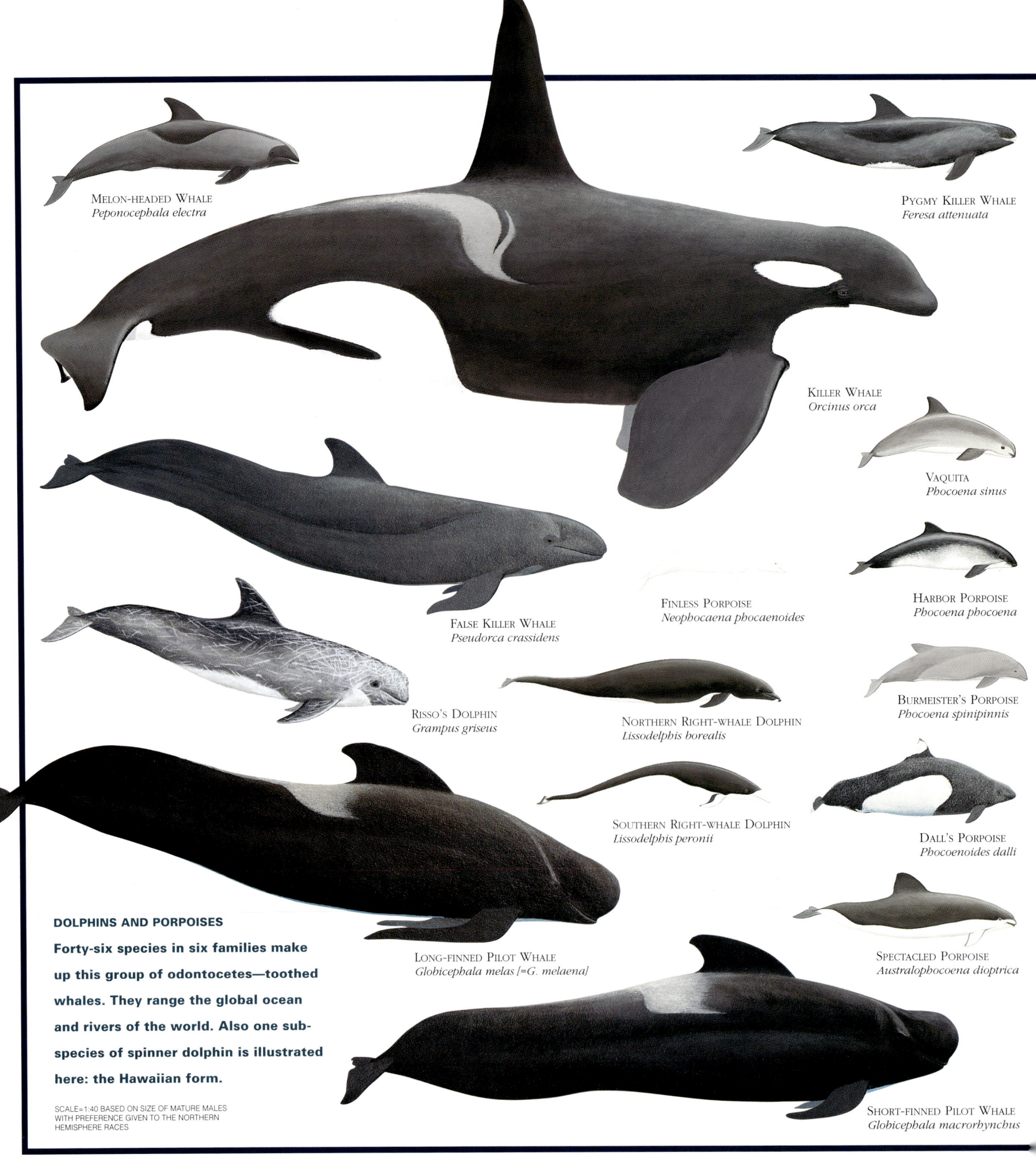

DOLPHINS AND PORPOISES

Forty-six species in six families make up this group of odontocetes—toothed whales. They range the global ocean and rivers of the world. Also one subspecies of spinner dolphin is illustrated here: the Hawaiian form.

SCALE=1:40 BASED ON SIZE OF MATURE MALES WITH PREFERENCE GIVEN TO THE NORTHERN HEMISPHERE RACES

THE FUTURE

--- CHAPTER FIVE ---

Charles "Flip" Nicklin

I AM HUDDLED IN THE SHALLOWS OF JOHNSTONE STRAIT OFF VANCOUVER ISLAND, BRITISH COLUMBIA, MY BACK TO THE ROCKS AS I TRY TO CATCH MY BREATH. THE WATER IS 45°F. I'M IN A DRY SUIT, WITH FINS, MASK, SNORKEL, AND WEIGHTS—PLUS A FRESHLY LOADED NIKONOS. THIS SITE IS A KNOWN "RUBBING BEACH" FOR KILLER WHALES. ANY MINUTE NOW, A BUNCH OF THEM COULD ROUND A NEARBY SPIT AND COME IN REALLY CLOSE. THEY'VE JUST HAD A GOOD FEED IN THE STRAIT, SO IT'S LIKELY. MY CHALLENGE IS TURNING THIS OPPORTUNITY INTO A QUALITY PHOTOGRAPH. KILLER WHALES CAN BE AWFULLY SHY WHEN WE HUMANS TRY TO JOIN THEM IN THE WATER. TODAY I'M HOPING THAT, BY GETTING IN BEFORE THEY ARRIVE, I'LL BE LESS OBTRUSIVE, MORE JUST A PART OF THEIR SURROUNDINGS. TIMING, I FIGURE, IS THE KEY.

FACING PAGE: *Captive beluga captivates a young visitor to the Vancouver Aquarium.*
PRECEDING PAGES: *Killer whales cleave placid waters in the Pacific Northwest.*
ANNIE GRIFFITHS BELT (FACING PAGE); KEN BALCOMB (PRECEDING PAGES)

OF DOG AND DOLPHIN
In Ireland's Dingle Bay a bottlenose dolphin known as Fungie and a terrier named Jock share an inexplicable bond. When Jock is aboard his owner's boat, Fungie often appears, even leaping over the bow as the terrier yaps in excitement. Not just a dog lover, Fungie also cavorts with humans, attracting tourists and helping raise local awareness of marine mammals and their needs. Bottlenose dolphins are a wide-ranging species, occuring from the North Sea to the Bahamas to New Zealand, living in many different marine habitats. Some, like Fungie, are loners that also harbor an interest in things human. Why they travel singly and why they seek out humans remain mysteries.

Perhaps—as Plutarch observed nearly two millennia ago, the dolphin "is the only creature who loves man for his own sake."

Following pages:
Steely light of early morning silhouettes bottlenose dolphin and man as they fish together in Milne Bay, Papua New Guinea. Here, as in some other areas, wild dolphins cooperate with local fishermen, at times leading them to schools of fish or even herding prey toward them and sharing in the take.

It won't be easy. For one thing, I can't see them coming, because the rocky spit blocks my view. I can't use scuba gear, because whales don't like the sound of scuba bubbles; they'd almost certainly avoid the area. My plan is to free dive, and that's where timing comes in: If I wait for the whales to show before I get into the water, they'll probably notice me and shy away. But if I submerge now, I could run out of air before they make their inshore move. Then I'd have to resurface—perhaps just as they come in—which also might make them scatter. After talking with researchers John K. B. Ford and Graeme Ellis, I figure my best hope is to crawl slowly toward the whales underwater just as they arrive, almost like stalking wild animals on land. To this end, John will serve as my eyes, watching the pod from shore.

Waiting can be 98 or 99 percent of a whale photographer's day. I check my gear one more time, somewhat semiconsciously. A shout from John snaps my mind to attention: "They're coming, they're coming!"

I start hyperventilating, saturating my lungs for the dive.

"No, they're not." False alarm. I still can't see the whales for the rocks, but I can hear them. They must be very close. They certainly take their time; we've been through this a few times already. I listen to the sounds of my own breathing and the water splashing. Then John yells again, and suddenly black-and-white shapes fill the shallows before me: Killer whales! I try to get a decent lungful of air—difficult with my heart in my throat—before dropping through water that is green but relatively clear today. The visibility is about 25 feet, the bottom only 6 or 8 feet down. As I slowly crawl toward the 20 or so whales, weeds and rocks abruptly give way to a bare area of smooth pebbles about the size and shape of M&Ms. They've been rubbed clean of any algae. I try to flatten myself into the stones. Please, please, you guys, come in close. Oh, and please don't eat me. I've seen what killer whales can do to seals and other marine mammals.

A large male appears out of the distant gloom and slides near, dragging first its side and then its back through the pebbles very sensuously, much like a bear scratching itself on a tree trunk. It comes within ten feet, yet it completely ignores me. Time seems drawn out in slow motion as I photograph him, then others, then suddenly realize that breathing again— SOON—is a priority. More seconds pass as I cautiously ease back to shore, still not wanting to disturb the whales. Then I'm out of the water, grinning. Though most of the roll in my camera remains unexposed, it will stay that way. The frames just shot are special—I know that even without seeing them—and they must be protected. I am amazed at my luck. I'm not really sure why the rubbing beach worked today, when at other times just having my feet in the water has caused whales to keep their distance. This was one of those rare moments when I was able to peek into the world of whales, make a picture, then jump back into my own world. It's been just a great day.

All this happened in 1981. I tried to swim with whales even before then—and I've been trying ever since. A good part of my life has been spent in dozens of remote camps and countless small boats, scattered from Sri Lanka to Patagonia to the Arctic ice pack. Following whales can be extremely frustrating, for they're seldom as cooperative as we would like. But on good days, those uncommonly good days, this is the best job in the world.

To slip into the water and be eye-to-eye with a whale is far more than a photo op. Such encounters never last long, and don't always yield memorable pictures. But things we see and experience underwater often go beyond the limits of the camera, at times becoming the material of dreams. My greatest dream is that we might someday swim with whales, not just for passing moments, but in more significant ways. I want to get to know them as well as we know cheetahs or bison or other land animals.

My family's interest in cetaceans goes back to 1963, when my father, Chuck Nicklin, "rode" a whale. A professional diver and underwater photographer, Chuck went scuba diving with some *(Continued on page 212)*

SAM ABELL, NGS PHOTOGRAPHER; DAVID DOUBILET (FOLLOWING PAGES)

FRANÇOIS GOHIER; FLIP NICKLIN / MINDEN PICTURES (ABOVE RIGHT)

MISSION OF MERCY

As the world watched in 1988, Inupiat whalers from Point Barrow, Alaska, worked with an international coalition to save three juvenile gray whales trapped by ice. Cutting a series of breathing holes with chain saws, they formed a path that lured the grays toward open water; Soviet icebreakers cleared the last segment. Two of the three whales made it to sea. For their part, the whalers saw no irony in their rescue efforts. "Whales are revered," one explained. "In the old days they meant survival to us." Still hunting bowheads today, Inupiat consider whaling critical to the preservation of their culture. Early on, boys in Barrow learn—by book (above) as well as by doing—to hunt and flense the giant creatures.

THE FUTURE

211

LEAP OF FAITH

Acrobatic harpooner uses strength, skill, and his own weight to drive a metal harpoon head into a sperm whale off Indonesia's Lembata Island. After a two-hour battle, his 30-foot-long quarry succumbed. Too heavy to drag ashore, it was beached by falling tides (below). Tradition-bound islanders such as these operate what is now the world's only shore-based hunt for sperm whales.

BON ISHIKAWA (BOTH)

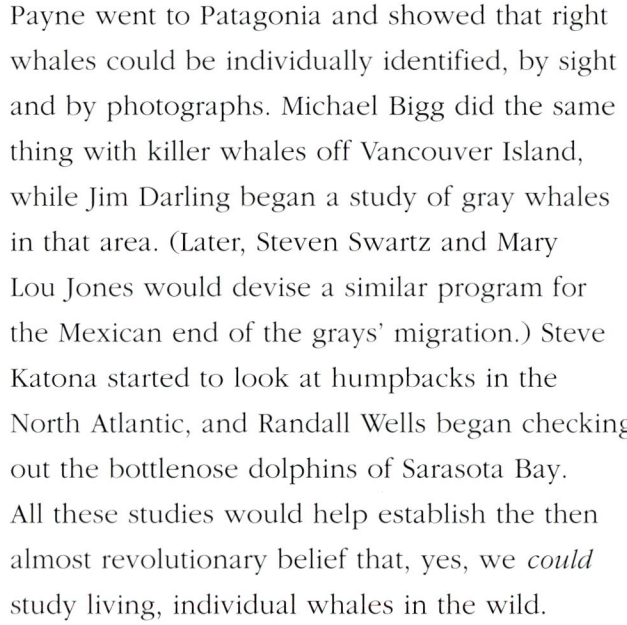

friends off San Diego one day. They happened on a fin whale, caught in the anchor line of a gill net. It would have died for sure if they hadn't set it free. And free it they did, after first taking some pictures of each other on its back. Those photos got on the wire services, and because it was a slow news day, they showed up across the country! Well, that chance encounter marked the beginning of a long-term relationship between my family and whales.

My father would go on to photograph many whale species in many situations, both stills and cinema. In time, so would I. Brother Terry also got into the act, helping to cut a net off a sperm whale in Sri Lanka. My mom, Gloria, was just happy we didn't try to bring any of our subjects home with us. That, at least, was a major improvement over my earlier interest in snakes.

In terms of studying cetaceans, the 1970s were seminal times. There was the growing environmental movement and the public's gradual awareness of the plight of whales. Also, whale research was just coming into its modern era. Scientists had long considered whales too difficult to study in the open ocean. Most of what they knew about them had come from whaling ships, companies, and commissions. But in the early seventies, Roger Payne went to Patagonia and showed that right whales could be individually identified, by sight and by photographs. Michael Bigg did the same thing with killer whales off Vancouver Island, while Jim Darling began a study of gray whales in that area. (Later, Steven Swartz and Mary Lou Jones would devise a similar program for the Mexican end of the grays' migration.) Steve Katona started to look at humpbacks in the North Atlantic, and Randall Wells began checking out the bottlenose dolphins of Sarasota Bay. All these studies would help establish the then almost revolutionary belief that, yes, we *could* study living, individual whales in the wild.

It was also in the early 1970s that NATIONAL GEOGRAPHIC began its modern coverage of wild whales. First was a gray whale story, followed by articles on right whales, all great whales, and then humpbacks. My father worked with undersea photographer Bill Curtsinger on some of them. Much of the time, he and Bill found themselves "chasing ghosts," in Bill's words. Little was known about where different species went or how they behaved. The challenge of photographing whales was awesome back then—it's pretty challenging even today—and often the only reward for weeks of work would be a single

STEVE MORGAN / GREENPEACE; MARK VOTIER / SYGMA (OPPOSITE)

glimpse of a fast-disappearing fluke. I can't give enough credit to guys like Bill and Chuck and Al Giddings and Flip Schulke and other pioneer whale photographers of the 1960s and 1970s—as well as to the scientists of that time—who had so little information and were just trying to find whales somewhere out in the big, blue sea.

I remember, every winter, gray whales would pass by my hometown of San Diego and we'd go watch their distant spouts from the Point Loma lighthouse. It was an annual ritual for us. Still, I had no overwhelming urge to photograph whales. The idea of swimming with them sounded interesting, but it seemed that pretty much everything that was doable had been done already. It also sounded incredibly frustrating.

My first whale photography job came in 1979, working with my father on a film about humpbacks, in Hawaii. The scientific advisor for that film was Jim Darling, and it soon became clear to me that everything *hadn't* been done with whales. Jim was very happy the day I was able to get some photos of a male humpback whose head was covered with bloody knobs. At that time, a lot of people thought of humpbacks as "gentle giants" that just cruised the oceans, peacefully filling up on plankton and never harming another living thing. Well, Jim had just discovered that humpbacks actually wage very dramatic battles at mating time, shoving and crashing into each other to gain access to the females. Not surprising, perhaps, when you consider that bighorn sheep and musk oxen do the same thing. But back then, the public had this misconception about whales—especially baleen whales—being docile and meek. Jim was studying real whales, and he was finding there was a lot more to being a humpback than just floating around, being gentle. Those bloody head knobs impressed me, too. Here at last was hard evidence, verifiable and possibly photographable. I sensed a turning point: I was becoming hooked on whales.

Two aspects of Jim's work especially moved me: The first was how careful and methodical he was; no jumping to conclusions from the few clues that turned up day to day. I also began to see that there were concrete things to look for, things that could be photographed to illustrate whale behavior and the new directions research was taking.

As the weeks passed in Hawaii, I met other young and enthusiastic biologists eager to study living whales, people like Peter Tyack, Ellie Dorsey, Debbie Glockner and her husband-to-be Mark Ferrari, Greg Silber, Graeme Ellis, and John Ford. It was an impressive group, with a wealth of ideas. Now they're nurturing an even larger, next generation of researchers. Today, the future of whales may not be clear, but whales definitely will be well studied.

In the last 16 years I've done 11 stories for NATIONAL GEOGRAPHIC. It has been immensely rewarding work. But my successes rely on years—often decades—of painstaking study by scientists, and I deeply thank them for sharing their findings so generously. I also owe sincere thanks to those experts who know whales from the perspective of the hunter. They possess generations of experience. In addition, they often have a good deal of concern over how they and their communities will be treated by my lens. Whale researchers or whale hunters, all my guides have spent much of their lives with their subjects, and it is they who make my pictures possible. To them all I am immensely grateful.

Public concern over whales often has focused on death by harpoon. "Save the Whales" campaigns have done a lot to raise our environmental and ethical consciousnesses. In the past, commercial whaling severely depleted

> Norway has chosen to ignore the moratorium because it feels the minke whale population it hunts is large enough to sustain continued harvests....

many species of great whales. But how important is it today? The hunting of great whales for profit has been under a moratorium by the International Whaling Commission since 1986. Some species, such as blue and humpback whales, have been totally protected since the mid-1960s; grays and rights have been off-limits even longer. Exceptions to the IWC ban include the taking of whales for "scientific study"—a provision currently used only by Japanese whalers, in their pursuit of minke whales. Norway has chosen to ignore the moratorium because it feels the minke whale population it hunts is large enough to sustain continued harvests at current levels. In addition, there are those who say that commercial whaling has been as important, historically, to the people of whaling nations as subsistence whaling has been to the Inupiat and other native peoples—whose whaling is permitted within limits set by the IWC.

Lately there is much talk of the IWC modifying the moratorium; some whale stocks seem to have recovered to the point where commercial and native interests may push for increased whaling. Yet even if this comes to pass, the impact of direct take on most cetaceans probably will be less significant—for the foreseeable future—than the effects of problems such as entanglement in nets, habitat loss, and pollution. Bycatch—the incidental death of whales and other nontarget animals in nets and traps intended for

STANDOFF AT SEA Greenpeace activists confront a Norwegian whaling vessel in 1994 (opposite), one year after Norway resumed commercial hunts for minke whales, smallest of the world's baleen whales. Norway filed a formal objection to the IWC moratorium on the commercial taking of all great whales, because it claims that minke populations in the northeastern Atlantic can sustain limited harvests. This stance and questions concerning the reliability of Norway's minke statistics have sparked international criticism— as has the pro-whaling agenda of Japan. Under an IWC provision, the Japanese continue to take up to 330 whales yearly, for "scientific purposes." The meat is processed and sold for human consumption, and scientists disagree over the merits of Japan's whale research.

Aboard a Japanese whaler working Antarctic waters, a crewman measures a minke fetus (below), one of 124 taken that season with

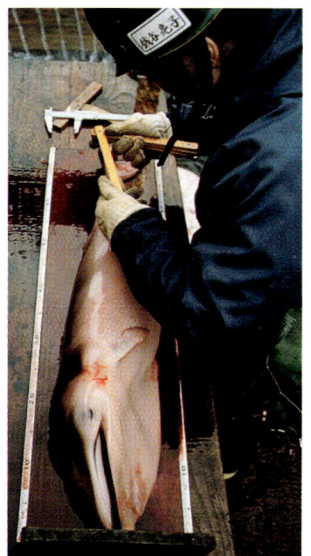

their mothers. Currently, Japan continues to wage aggressive campaigns within the IWC to justify its type of research and to modify the existing moratorium at least as it applies to minkes.

THE FUTURE

PERIL OF DEATH
Snagged on a sperm whale's lower jaw, a fragment of drift net trails the behemoth like a shadow. It creates considerable drag, and should it tangle on some undersea obstacle, the animal could drown. Whales and dolphins apparently cannot detect such monofilament nets with their eyes or their echolocation systems. A 1992 United Nations ban on drift-netting in the high seas has helped reduce whale deaths, but the danger persists. Discarded fragments of net can last for years, hampering and drowning marine mammals long after the fishermen who set them have gone.

FLIP NICKLIN / MINDEN PICTURES

fish—has claimed a million dolphins and porpoises per year in some years. While some of those animals were used for food, the vast majority were simply thrown back into the sea. Images of net-drowned dolphins contributed to the international ban on giant drift nets, instituted in 1992.

The past decade has witnessed a number of cetacean die-offs as well, quite apart from those deaths resulting from entanglement. In 1987-88, 14 humpbacks died and washed up on the northeastern U.S. coast—compared to just several known humpback deaths in the entire previous decade. In 1990-91, more than a thousand striped dolphin carcasses were found on the shores of the Mediterranean. While a virus was the immediate cause of death in that occurrence, necropsies showed that the animals contained levels of PCBs that were 10 to 50 times greater than what is considered dangerous to humans. They also were tainted with mercury and other toxins.

Today, belugas of the St. Lawrence River are in a virtual state of siege. Nonstop traffic, especially of small craft, means intense noise pollution for these echolocating mammals, while municipalities and industries dump varied wastes containing any number of poisons. Some substances banned decades ago are so long-lived that they still show up in the food chain. Local belugas and certain fish species are experiencing tumors, reproductive anomalies, and other problems.

Belugas are curious animals. Whenever I've been in the water with them, they always gather about to investigate my awkward presence. Their clicks and squeaks seem to intrigue everyone lucky enough to be within range. Early sailors heard belugas through the hulls of their ships, and called them sea canaries. Today, as in the past, Inuit kayakers listen to these cetaceans simply by putting ear to a partly submerged paddle. Considering the traditional use of canaries by human miners, shouldn't we worry when our marine "canaries" go quiet?

Whale biologist Steve Katona warns: "Whales are a barometer of the state of the ocean. They integrate what is going on over a long period of time and over great distances. They can tell us important things. We have to be sensitive and clever to learn what they can teach us, but the message is there. If the whales are having troubles, the ocean is having troubles, and if the ocean is having troubles, we are having troubles."

Whales and dolphins can thrive only in healthy environments, ones that are free of poisons, quiet enough for echolocation, and rich in needed prey species. Killer whales off the Pacific Northwest rely chiefly on local salmon; that salmon fishery is in trouble, so killer whales there also could be in trouble. In China, the baiji, or Yangtze River dolphin, is especially endangered: The damming of tributaries has all but destroyed its habitat, while an illegal, "rolling hook" fishery causes a major bycatch problem. Growing boat traffic and burgeoning human populations at *(Continued on page 222)*

DISPLACED DOLPHINS
Captive tucuxi in an artificial Brazilian lake nears a paddleboat of tourists. This species of dolphin inhabits rivers and coastal marine waters of South and Central America. Though not generally hunted, tucuxis are killed accidentally in fishnets. In addition, they face a major potential threat: a series of dams planned for the Amazon's numerous tributaries. Similar dams in Pakistan have brought the Indus River dolphin to the verge of extinction. Of all cetaceans, river dolphins are considered the most threatened. Their inland and coastal habitats, easily impacted, leave them especially vulnerable to the varied effects of fishing, pollution, damming, and other human activities.

Following pages:
Long of beak and small of eye, a captive boto roams a man-made lake in the Brazilian town of Lagoa da Prata, after being rescued from a drying irrigation ditch. At home in major rivers of the Amazon and Orinoco basins, botos rely heavily on echolocation to maneuver and to find fish in the often murky waters. Noise pollution from human river traffic can severely affect their ability to echolocate.

FLIP NICKLIN / MINDEN PICTURES
(ABOVE AND FOLLOWING PAGES)

THE FUTURE

BACK TO NATURE?

Sea of smiles all but surrounds a bottlenose dolphin named Misha as handlers return him to his native Tampa Bay. Captive for two years, he took part in a University of California experimental program focusing on echolocation research. The project also addressed a vital question: Could dolphins removed from the wild successfully readapt to the rigors of the natural world? In Misha's case, the answer seems to be yes. But not all dolphins receive the meticulous planning and consideration involved with this particular program, and controversy rages over which captive animals should be set free. Another concern: humanity's continuing alteration of marine habitats. Bottlenose dolphins leap in the wake of shrimp boats despite the pollution and industrial noise of the Galveston ship channel (above). High levels of PCBs and mercury have been found in beached Texas dolphins.

THE FUTURE

riverside have meant more and more pollution, noise, and boat-dolphin collisions, as well as sharp declines in the baiji's prey fish. There is a good chance that this will be the first cetacean in modern times to go extinct. Other river dolphin species, in South America and India, also are at risk. Around the world, direct and indirect damage to habitat and exploitation by various fisheries seriously threaten the future of many cetaceans.

Whale research always has focused on numbers. Scientists began by counting whales—dead ones, initially, because they were so much easier to count than living ones. But as researchers' technologies improved, so did the accuracy of their estimates of live populations. Techniques also became less invasive; Discovery Tags—metal identification tubes embedded in the blubber and muscle of living whales—in time gave way to photographic identification and other, more benign procedures. Along the way we've found cetaceans to be an interesting lot, from huge blue whales to bizarre river dolphins. We've learned to recognize different individuals within each study group. We've improved our understanding of their ages and reproductive rates, thanks to work like Roger Payne's right whale studies in Patagonia and to Randall Wells's bottlenose dolphin research in Sarasota Bay. Their methods, such as photographic identification, transect line surveys, and whale tracking

FLIP NICKLIN (ABOVE); FLIP NICKLIN / MINDEN PICTURES (UPPER AND OPPOSITE)

with hydrophones, have become standard. Now Hal Whitehead and others are venturing farther out, with boats full of increasingly sophisticated equipment. In time, they or those who come after may count and track whales from space stations or submarines, using remote-sensing gear and undersea acoustic arrays. Others may one day establish complete family trees for cetaceans, through DNA obtained from bits of skin sloughed off by passing animals.

Still, research on wild whales is relatively new; it's been only 23 years since NATIONAL GEOGRAPHIC first visited Roger Payne in Patagonia. Cetaceans seem to be fairly long-lived—some are in the human range, though we still don't know life expectancies for many species—and so researchers have yet to monitor a single generation of wild whales through a complete life cycle. In time they will. While counting individuals and identifying discrete stocks will continue to be a large part of whale research, I think it safe to say that we are just beginning to study whales beyond the basic numbers: their population sizes, reproduction rates, calving intervals, life expectancies, and such.

In 1979, blue and bowhead whales both seemed doomed; I never expected to see—much less photograph—either. Yet today we have a growing understanding of both species, thanks largely to two of the most exciting technological developments in cetacean studies. The first, satellite telemetry, seems like something out of *Star Trek* but is very real. Small transmitters are attached to whales; they beam signals to orbiting communications satellites, which in turn relay coded information to researchers thousands of miles away. Such transmitters can be used to plot an animal's location and course. But they are much more than locator beacons. They also give us behavioral

DOLPHINS GALORE
New Zealand's waters provide fertile ground both for cetaceans and for those who study them. Marine biologist Bernd Würsig tracks dusky dolphins off Kaikoura, on the South Island (above). Farther out, deep submarine canyons harbor fish and squid favored by sperm whales, which support Kaikoura's burgeoning whale-watching economy (opposite, upper). Lucky passengers aboard one cruise stare as a male subadult sperm begins its headlong dive into the deep (opposite, lower). Growing rapidly worldwide, whale-watching now attracts millions of people yearly. While many scientists feel such cruises enhance public sensitivity to marine mammals, others question the effects on the animals themselves.

> EVEN FOLLOWING CETACEANS IN SMALL BOATS...CAN DISRUPT THE NORMAL BEHAVIOR OF WHALE AND DOLPHIN GROUPS. OFTEN, THE EFFECTS CAN BE CUMULATIVE....

insights, for they can report how deep and often an individual whale dives, and they can monitor heart rate and other physiological parameters as a creature swims, dives, feeds, or mates. Already this technology has been used successfully with bowheads, humpbacks, and blue whales, with sperm whales, belugas, and pilot whales, and each year the transmitters get smaller and more efficient, the batteries more powerful. Satellite tracking is especially

THE FUTURE

exciting because it permits the remote sensing of whale activities at depth and gives a more complete picture of whale life in the wild.

A second technique, acoustic tracking, consists of following whales by monitoring the sounds they make. With this method, Cornell University's Christopher W. Clark has been able to differentiate individuals and to revolutionize the counting of bowheads off northern Alaska. Just as a recording studio uses arrays of microphones, headsets, and speakers to divide and recombine the soundtracks of different musicians, Chris envisions wiring the oceans with arrays of hydrophones that will enable scientists to track the movements of different whale groups, worldwide. Sound futuristic? It's already begun. Its centerpiece is the U.S. Navy's undersea tracking network, originally devised to detect enemy submarines. While turning the ocean into one huge sound studio presents some gigantic challenges—how to handle the natural "noise" of other marine life, for example—humpbacks, blues, and other species already are being successfully monitored through a realm that is much too vast to survey any other way.

Yet another promising tool is DNA technology, which will help researchers determine different stocks within a single population, as well as evolutionary interrelationships among different whale species. In addition, the establishment of genetic fingerprints for each species will mean that inspectors will be able to tell whether whale meat has been taken legally or from protected animals. All in all, we're living in an interesting period of marine mammal study.

There is, of course, a cost whenever humans interfere with whale societies. It is most obvious when animals are actually removed from wild populations, whether through hunting, bycatch, or even live capture. There also are costs when we influence cetaceans in nonlethal ways. Those who work regularly with whales, whether scientists or photographers like myself, generally are very concerned that the impact of their actions upon whales be minimal. They constantly question themselves: Are the potential gains of their work worth the costs? Some data-gathering techniques are more invasive than others. Satellite rigs and video cameras mounted on subject animals involve physical contact and, possibly, physical discomfort, so responsible researchers use them cautiously. Even following cetaceans in small boats—to make identification photos or just to

WHALE'S-EYE VIEW
Holding a deepwater video probe, researcher Iain Kerr of the Whale Conservation Institute plans to explore the sperm whale's realm remotely, by attaching probes to his subjects with suction cups.

whale-watch—can disrupt the normal behavior of whale and dolphin groups. Often, the effects can be cumulative; while a single boat of whale-watchers off Hawaii probably has next to no impact, a thousand boats would be a disaster. Again, what is the gain, and is it worth the cost?

Today, the Johnstone Strait rubbing beaches where I first swam with killer whales are protected; no one can disturb the animals. Photographers now must plan ahead, setting up cameras long before the whales arrive, triggering them remotely, then recovering them after the creatures leave. It's a bit more involved, not as physically thrilling as being in the middle of the action, but it's certainly a lot less disruptive to the whales.

Cetaceans continue to fascinate us, as they have for centuries. We've read *Moby Dick*, watched Flipper on television, seen Willy at the movies, listened to records of whale songs, met Shamu at Sea World, and cruised in whale-watch tourboats—sometimes in the very places where hunting whales once was a major industry. We're even starting to swim with wild dolphins and whales. It is hard for us to follow them, to see them dive from view, and not to wonder. They still prompt more questions than answers.

Do sperm whales really have epic battles with giant squid? What do they use their huge brains for? What do they do at those impossible depths, so alien to our world? Do other, yet undiscovered, deepwater whales also exist? Where do blue whales have their young? How is it that dolphins can rest one side of their brains at a time, and how intelligent are they, really?

I know of no more inspirational cetacean study than Denise Herzing's Wild Dolphin Project. For more than a decade now, she and her associates have been doing what are known as "focal follows" of spotted dolphins in the waters between Florida and the Bahamas. For a week at a time, they anchor on a shallow bank and wait for dolphins to come to them. Most days, the animals do just that. On the best days, they permit Denise to swim with them for extended periods, and even slow their pace to enable her to keep up. She videotapes their behavior and records their sounds, usually focusing on a particular individual. The dolphins seem curious yet relaxed. It is exciting work—for these are wild creatures, living apparently normal cetacean lives, feeding, mating, and caring for their young.

There is a hope that the future will offer opportunities to accompany other species as well. Will we someday swim with wild killer whales as we have begun to do with humpbacks and dolphins? Will new generations of small submersibles and other machinery eventually enable us to roam with sperm whales at their awesome depths? Even if we manage to follow those dramatic flukes far beneath the waves, even if we record the entire spectrum of their mysterious chirps and clicks, will we ever truly know these creatures? Many of our questions must wait, perhaps for other people in other times to answer them. Indeed, I think we've only just begun to swim with whales.

FIELD TECHNOLOGIES
Near Barrow, Alaska, whale researcher Mari Smultea precisely plots positions of different animals with a surveyor's theodolite, later extrapolating directions and rates of travel. Off the Galápagos, sperm whale expert Hal Whitehead's three-year-old daughter, Stefanie, listens in on whale vocalizations via hydrophones. Such techniques have helped increase our knowledge of whales.

Following pages:
A researcher hovers near a humpback calf off the west coast of Maui. As scientists continue to swim with whales, both humans and whales may gain new perspectives.

FLIP NICKLIN / MINDEN PICTURES (ALL); DEBORAH A. GLOCKNER-FERRARI / CENTER FOR WHALE STUDIES (FOLLOWING PAGES)

THE FUTURE

Cetaceans

Mysticetes

GRAY WHALE
Eschrichtius robustus
b: 4.6 m, 500 kg; sm: ♀ 11.7 m, ♂ 11.1 m; pm: ♀ 14.1 m, ♂ 13 m, 26–31,000 kg; mx: ♀ 15 m, ♂ 14.6 m, 34,000 kg.
f: many varieties of benthic amphipods, isopods, polychaetes, tubeworms.
d: coastal N. Pacific, Korea to Okhotsk Sea, Bering Sea to Baja California.
s: extinct in Atlantic; Korean stock endangered; stable in eastern N. Pacific.

NORTHERN RIGHT WHALE
Eubalaena glacialis
b: 4.8–6 m; sm: ♀ 15.5 m, ♂ 15 m; mx: ≈54,000 kg; ♀ 18.3 m, ♂ 16.4 m.
f: zooplankton, favoring copepods.
d: Northern cool temperate to subarctic waters near continental shore.
s: endangered; N. Pacific, near extinction; N. Atlantic, a few hundred left.

SOUTHERN RIGHT WHALE
Eubalaena australis
b: 4.5–6.0 m; mx: ♀ 16.5 m, ♂ 15.2 m
f: zooplankton, euphausiids, copepods.
d: circumpolar Southern Hemisphere from 20°S to 55°S, sometimes to 63°S.
s: vulnerable, fully protected.

BOWHEAD WHALE
Balaena mysticetus
b: 3.5–4.5 m; sm: ♀ 14–15.2 m, ♂ 12 m; pm: ♀ 17–18 m, ♂ 14–15 m, 75,000 kg; mx: ♀ 20 m, ♂ 18 m, to 110,000 kg.
f: euphausiids, some copepods, swimming mollusks and sea jellies.
d: restricted to Arctic and subarctic waters, at or near pack ice, up leads.
s: vulnerable (formerly endangered).

PYGMY RIGHT WHALE
Caperea marginata
b: 2 m; sm: ♀ <6 m; pm: ♀ 6.45 m, ♂ 6.09 m; mx: ♀ 6.45 m; ♂ 6.09 m
f: copepods, other crustaceans.
d: circumpolar Southern Hemisphere from 31°S to 52°S.
s: insufficiently known, protected.

MINKE WHALE
Balaenoptera acutorostrata
b: 2.4–2.84 m; sm: ♀ 7.5 m, ♂ 6.7–7.0 m; pm: ♀ 8.5 m, ♂ 7.9 m, 5,800–7,200 kg; mx: ♀ 10.7 m; ♂ 9.8 m (N. Pacific 9.2 m); northern ≈15% smaller than southern.
f: skimmer/gulper taking a variety of invertebrates and schooling fish.
d: cosmopolitan, Arctic to Antarctic.
s: insufficiently known, many taken directly and in "scientific whaling."

BRYDE'S WHALE
Balaenoptera edeni
b: ≈3.4 m; sm: ♀ 12.5 m, ♂ 12.2 m; avg: ♀ ≈13 m, ♂ ≈12 m at 12,000 kg; mx: ♀ 15.5 m, ♂ 14.3 m to 20,000 kg.
f: lunges for fish and krill.
d: tropical and subtropical regions below 40° of both hemispheres.
s: insufficiently known, exploitable.

SEI WHALE
Balaenoptera borealis
b: 4.6 m; sm: (N/S) ♀ 13.4/ 14 m, ♂ 12.8/13.5 m; pm: (N/S) ♀ 18.6/21 m, ♂ 17/17.7 m; mx: ♀ 21 m, ♂ 18.5 m.
f: skimmer for copepods, amphipods, euphausiids, small fish, squid.
d: most oceans, tropics to subpolar seas, prefers temperate pelagic waters.
s: vulnerable; harvested until 1977.

FIN WHALE
Balaenoptera physalus
b: 6–6.5 m; sm: (N/S) ♀ 18.3/19.9 m, ♂ 17.7/19.2 m, at 35,000–45,000 kg; mx: (N/S) ♀ 24/27 m, ♂ 22/25 m.
f: small schooling fish and invertebrates (especially euphausiids), also copepods and squid.
d: all oceans, warm temperate waters in winter, polar regions in summer.
s: vulnerable, profoundly affected by whaling, apparently not recovering.

BLUE WHALE
Balaenoptera musculus
b: 6–7 m; sm: N♀ 21–23 m, N♂ 20–21 m; S♀ 23–24 m, S♂ 22 m; pm: N♀ 25 m, N♂ 24 m; S♀ 26–27 m, S♂ 24–25 m to about 130,000 kg;
mx: S♀ 33.58 m, S♂ 31 m, N♂ 26.2 m; pygmy form ≈20% smaller.
f: mostly euphausiids, some squid, copepods, amphipods, red crabs.
d: winter toward tropics; cool temperate zones to edge of pack ice in summer, others year-round residents.
s: endangered; Antarctic stocks now less than 0.3% of original numbers.

HUMPBACK WHALE
Megaptera novaeangliae
b: 4.5–5 m; sm: ♀ 11–12 m, ♂ 11–11.5 m; mx: ♀ 19 m, ♂ 17.5 m; 40,000-48,000 kg; northern race smaller.
f: various small fish and invertebrates.
d: cosmopolitan, usually feeds in cold temperate waters, breeds in tropics.
s: vulnerable, severely reduced by whaling, showing signs of recovery.

Odontocetes

SPERM WHALE
Physeter macrocephalus
b: ≈4 m; sm: ♀ 8.3–9.2 m, ♂ 11–12 m; pm: ♀ 11–12 m at 20,000 kg, ♂ 15–18 m at 36,000 kg; mx: ♀ 17 m to 38,000 kg, ♂ 20 m, to ≈ 52,000 kg.
f: large pelagic squid, other cephalopods, medium to large fish.
d: all deep oceans from the Antarctic across the Equator to the Arctic.
s: insufficiently known; depleted by whaling, apparently not in danger.

PYGMY SPERM WHALE
Kogia breviceps
b: ≈1.2 m at 55 kg; sm: ♀ 2.6–2.9 m, ♂ 2.7–3.0 m; mx: 3.4 m, 408 kg.
f: abyssal cephalopods (squid, octopus), fish and benthic invertebrates.
d: nearly all tropical to temperate deep waters around the world.
s: insufficiently known, apparently stable and unthreatened.

DWARF SPERM WHALE
Kogia simus
b: ≈1.0 m at 46 kg; sm: 2.1–2.2 m, 154 kg; mx: 2.7 m, 272 kg.
f: abyssal cephalopods (squid and octopus), fish, benthic invertebrates.
d: nearly all tropical to temperate deep waters around the world.
s: insufficiently known, but apparently stable and unthreatened.

CUVIER'S BEAKED WHALE
Ziphius cavirostris
b: 2.1–2.7 m; sm: ♀ 5.12 m, ♂ 5.26 m; mx: ♀ 6.6 m, ♂ 6.93 m, ≈3,000 kg.
f: deep pelagic cephalopods, also some fish and crustaceans.
d: tropical to cold temperate deep waters of all oceans.
s: insufficiently known, no threats.

SHEPHERD'S BEAKED WHALE
Tasmacetus shepherdi
Of 11 known records only 4 have been measured—2 ♂s at 6.4 m and 7.0 m, and 2 ♀s, at 6.0 m and 6.6 m
f: probably benthic deepwater fish.
d: known only from southernmost Australia, South America (Argentina and Chile), and New Zealand.
s: insufficiently known, quite rare.

NORTHERN BOTTLENOSE WHALE
Hyperoodon ampullatus
b: ≈3.5 m; sm: ♀ 6.0 m, ♂ 7.3 m; pm: ♀ 7.5 m, ≈3,000 kg, ♂ 9.1 m, ≈3,600 kg; mx: ♀ 8.7 m, ♂ 9.8 m.
f: mostly squid, but also some benthic fish and invertebrates.
d: deep cold temperate to subarctic North Atlantic waters.
s: insufficiently known, reduced well below pre-whaling abundance.

SOUTHERN BOTTLENOSE WHALE
Hyperoodon planifrons
b: 2.75–2.91 m; sm: ♀ <5.7 m, ♂ >5.2 m; mx: ♀ 7.8 m, ♂ 7.14 m; <4,000 kg.
f: primarily deepwater squid.
d: circumpolar south of about 30°S to Antarctica.
s: insufficiently known, rarely seen.

BAIRD'S BEAKED WHALE
Berardius bairdii
b: ≈4.5 m; sm: ♀ 9.8–10.6 m, ♂ 9.1–9.7 m; 9,000 kg;
mx: ♀ 12.8 m, ♂ 11.9 m.
f: benthic cephalopods, crustaceans, and fish.
d: deep warm to cold temperate waters across the North Pacific.
s: insufficiently known, not rare, not covered by whaling moratorium.

ARNOUX'S BEAKED WHALE
Berardius arnuxii
few specimens have been measured.
b: ≈3.5 m; mx: ♀ 9.8 m, ♂ 9.6 m; to about 6,500 kg.
f: benthic cephalopods, pelagic fish, and crustaceans.
d: circumpolar deep cold temperate to Antarctic waters of the Southern Hemisphere.
s: insufficiently known.

BLAINVILLE'S BEAKED WHALE
Mesoplodon densirostris
b: 2.0–2.4 m, mx: ♀ 4.7 m, ♂ 5.9 m, to 1,033 kg.
f: benthic cephalopods.
d: wide distribution across all temperate and tropical deep waters.
s: insufficiently known, relatively common for a beaked whale.

ANDREWS' BEAKED WHALE
Mesoplodon bowdoini
few specimens actually measured
b: ≈2 m; mx: ♀ 4.57 m; ♂ 4.67 m.
f: unknown, probably pelagic squid.
d: southern temperate waters near Australia, Tasmania, New Zealand.
s: insufficiently known, very rare.

HUBBS' BEAKED WHALE
Mesoplodon carlhubbsi
possibly a northern subspecies of Andrew's beaked whale.
b: ≈2.5 m; pm: 4.88–4.96 m; mx: ♀ 5.32 m; ♂ 5.32 m; 1,500 kg.
f: squid and some mesopelagic fish.
d: cool temperate eastern North Pacific from about 54°N to 32°N on the American side and off northeastern Japan (38°N), unknown in between.
s: insufficiently known, uncommon.

GINKGO-TOOTHED BEAKED WHALE
Mesoplodon ginkgodens
b: ≈2 m; mx: ♀ 4.9 m, ♂ 4.77 m to ≈1,500 kg (few measured).
f: unknown, but probably squid.
d: 18 known specimens scattered over warm temperate and tropical Pacific and Indian Oceans, Sri Lanka to Southern California.
s: insufficiently known, rare.

STEJNEGER'S BEAKED WHALE
Mesoplodon stejnegeri
b: 2.45 m; mx: ♀/♂ 5.25 m, 1,200 kg.
f: squid.
d: cold temperate to subarctic waters of the North Pacific continental slope from California to Sea of Japan.
s: insufficiently known, very rare.

GRAY'S BEAKED WHALE
Mesoplodon grayi
b: < 2.37 m; mx: ♀ 5.33 m, ♂ 5.64 m
f: probably squid.
d: cool temperate circumpolar Southern Hemisphere oceans.
s: insufficiently known, rare.

GERVAIS' BEAKED WHALE
Mesoplodon europaeus
b: 1.96–2.2 m; sm: ♀ 4.5 m; mx: ♀ 5.2 m, ♂ 4.56 m, to >1,200 kg.
f: squid.
d: warm temperate, tropical Atlantic, mostly in Gulf of Mexico, Caribbean, and eastern North American coast.
s: insufficiently known.

SOWERBY'S BEAKED WHALE
Mesoplodon bidens
b: <2.40 m; pm: ♀ 5.1 m, ♂ 5.5 m, to ≈1,250 kg (few measured).
f: squid and small fish.
d: across the cold temperate North Atlantic, especially the North Sea.
s: insufficiently known, rare.

TRUE'S BEAKED WHALE
Mesoplodon mirus
b: ≈2.33 m; mx: ♀ 5.1 m; ♂ 5.33 m, to 1,400 kg.
f: squid.
d: ≈ 30 strandings scattered from Great Britain to eastern North America, South Africa to Australia.
s: insufficiently known, rare.

HECTOR'S BEAKED WHALE
Mesoplodon hectori
b: 1.9–2.1 m; mx: ♀ 4.43 m; ♂ 4.34 m.
f: squid, probably some invertebrates.
d: known from 24 S. Hemisphere strandings scattered from South America, South Africa to Australia.
s: insufficiently known, very rare.

PYGMY BEAKED WHALE
Mesoplodon peruvianus
b: 1.6 m; mx: 3.7 m, <1,000 kg.
f: squid, crustaceans, small fish.
d: eastern tropical Pacific from Peru so. of 8°S to southern Baja California.
s: insufficiently known, rare, taken incidentally in drift-net fisheries.

LONGMAN'S BEAKED WHALE
Mesoplodon pacificus
Beyond only two weathered skulls from northeastern Australia and Somalia virtually nothing is known. Size is estimated at up to 7.5 m.
s: insufficiently known, very rare.

STRAP-TOOTHED WHALE
Mesoplodon layardii
b: 2.2–2.8 m; mx: ♀ 6.15 m, ♂ 5.84 m.
f: squid.
d: cold temperate circumpolar Southern Hemisphere seas.
s: insufficiently known, rare.

MESOPLODON SPECIES A
Mesoplodon sp.
Seen relatively often, but not handled. No specimens currently exist.
pm: 5.5 m (estimated)
f: unknown, but probably squid.
d: eastern tropical Pacific from Peru to Baja California, Mexico.
s: insufficiently known, rare.

SUSU (GANGES RIVER DOLPHIN)
Platanista gangetica
b: 0.65–0.9 m; sm: ♀ 2 m, ♂ 1.7 m; ≈35–44 kg; pm: ♀ 2.5 m, ♂ 2.1 m; mx: ♀ 2.52 m, ♂ 2.12 m; 108 kg.
f: various freshwater fish, crustaceans.
d: from the mouths to headwaters of the Ganges, Brahmaputra, Karnaphuli, and Meghna Rivers (southern Asia).
s: vulnerable; greaty reduced.

BHULAN (INDUS RIVER DOLPHIN)
Platanista minor
b: 0.7–0.9 m; sm: ♀ 2 m, ♂ 1.7 m; pm: ♀ 2.5 m, ♂ 2.1 m; ≈100 kg.
f: various freshwater fish, crustaceans.
d: formerly the entire Indus River, now 80% are confined to 170 km in Pakistan between 2 irrigation barrages.
s: endangered, ≈ 500 animals left.

BAIJI (YANGTZE RIVER DOLPHIN)
Lipotes vexillifer
b: 0.7–0.9 m; sm: ♀ >2.0 m, ♂ 1.9–2.1 m; pm: ♀ 2.5 m, ♂ 2.16 m; 72–120 kg; mx: ♀ 2.53 m; ♂ 2.3 m; 167 kg.
f: small freshwater fish.
d: Yangtze River (China).
s: endangered; 150–300 left and declining; near its genetic threshold.

BOTO (AMAZON RIVER DOLPHIN)
Inia geoffrensis
b: 0.8 m; sm: ♀ 1.6–1.75 m, ♂ >1.98 m; pm: ♀ 1.96 m, ♂ 2.55 m; ≈96.5 kg; mx: ♀ 2.28 m, ♂ 2.74 m; 160 kg.
f: a wide variety of small freshwater fish, often characinid fish (tetras)
d: common at confluences of the Orinoco and Amazon River basins.
s: vulnerable, based on existing ecological threats to the Amazon River basin.

FRANCISCANA (LA PLATA DOLPHIN)
Pontoporia blainvillei
b: ≈0.75 m; sm: ♀ 1.37–1.47 m, ♂ 1.21–1.37 m; pm: ♀ 1.7 m, ♂ 1.5 m; mx: ♀ 1.77 m, 34 kg, ♂ 1.63 m, 29 kg.
f: bottom-feeding fish, shrimp, squid.
d: Atlantic coast of South America, from Brazil to Argentina
s: insufficiently known; huge incidental take in gill nets raises concern.

TUCUXI
Sotalia fluviatilis
estuarine form: b: 0.6–0.65 m; sm: ♀ 1.6–1.7 m; mx: 2.1 m, 50 kg.
riverine form: b: 0.71–0.83 m; sm: ♀ 1.32–1.37 m; mx: 1.6 m, 40 kg.
f: characoid fish in rivers; pelagic and demersal fish, squid along the coast.
d: riverine in Orinoco and Amazon River basins; estuarine and nearshore along the tropical Atlantic coast of South America.
s: insufficiently known, subject to threats to the Amazon ecosystem.

INDO-PACIFIC HUMP-BACKED DOLPHIN
Sousa chinensis
b: 0.98 m; mx: ♀ 2.44 m, ♂ 3.2 m.
f: nearshore fish, crustaceans, and mollusks.
d: coastal waters of the central western Pacific and Indian Oceans, Australia to South Africa (especially near mangroves).
s: insufficiently known.

Atlantic Hump-backed Dolphin
Sousa teuszii
b: ≈ 0.9 m; sm: ♂ 2 m;
mx: ♀ 2.35m, ♂ 2.48 m; 284 kg.
f: schooling coastal fish (mullet).
d: coastal, possibly riverine, equatorial to subtropical West Africa.
s: insufficiently known; direct and incidental takes probably occur.

Rough-toothed Dolphin
Steno bredanensis
b: 0.88 m; sm: ♀ 2.31 m, ♂ 2.2 m;
mx: ♀ 2.55 m, ♂ 2.65 m to 150 kg.
f: pelagic cephalopods and fish.
d: mostly pelagic tropical to warm temperate waters around the world.
s: insufficiently known; it appears to be naturally not abundant.

Bottlenose Dolphin
Tursiops truncatus
b: 0.84–1.22 m; sm: ♀ 2.33–3.12 m, ♂ 2.39–2.83 m; mx: ♀ 3.67 m, ♂ 3.81 m; >650 kg. At least three distinct forms exist.
f: fish, cephalopods, invertebrates.
d: tropical to temperate coastal and inshore waters worldwide.
s: insufficiently known; common.

Atlantic White-sided Dolphin
Lagenorhynchus acutus
b: 1.1–1.2 m; sm: ♀ 1.94–2.22 m, ♂ 2.1–2.4 m; mx: ♀ 2.43 m, 182 kg; ♂ 2.75 m, 235 kg.
f: various small fish, squid, shrimp.
d: the cold temperate North Atlantic.
s: insufficiently known; no threats.

White-beaked Dolphin
Lagenorhynchus albirostris
b: ≈1.2 m; sm: ♀ 2.5 m, ♂ 2.5–2.6 m;
mx: ♀ 3.05 m, ♂ 3.15 m; 275 kg.
f: cephalopods, pelagic schooling fish, some benthic crustaceans.
d: cold temperate to subarctic waters of the North Atlantic.
s: insufficiently known; no threats.

Pacific White-sided Dolphin
Lagenorhynchus obliquidens
b: 1–1.24 m; sm: ♀ 1.7–2.2 m, ♂ 1.7–2 m; mx: ♀ 2.36 m, ♂ 2.5 m; 180 kg.
f: pelagic schooling fish and squid.
d: across the cool temperate N. Pacific.
s: insufficiently known; caught incidentally in pelagic net fisheries.

Dusky Dolphin
Lagenorhynchus obscurus
b: 0.55–0.7 m; mx: ♀ 1.93 m, ♂ 2.11 m; 40–80 kg.
f: mainly anchovy, benthic fish, squid.
d: coastal warm to cold temperate waters in the Southern Hemisphere, especially South Africa, New Zealand, and South America.
s: insufficiently known; certain local populations under severe threat from direct and illegal fisheries.

Hourglass Dolphin
Lagenorhynchus cruciger
b: <1 m; mx: ♀ 1.83 m, ♂ 1.63 m, ≈50–60 kg (few have been measured).
f: small pelagic fish.
d: circumpolar pelagic cold temperate to Antarctic waters (S. Hemisphere).
s: insufficiently known; no threats.

Peale's Dolphin
Lagenorhynchus australis
b: <1 m; avg: 2 m; mx: 2.16 m to about 115 kg (few measured).
f: small fish and cephalopods.
d: coastal southernmost S. America.
s: insufficiently known; subject to significant impact from illegal bait fisheries in Chile and Argentina.

Fraser's Dolphin
Lagenodelphis hosei
b: 0.95–1.1 m; sm: ♀<2.1 m, ♂<2.3 m;
mx: 2.64 m, 210 kg.
f: mesopelagic fish, shrimp, squid; possibly benthic prey as well.
d: all pelagic subtropical through equatorial waters from 30°N to 30°S.
s: insufficiently known; stable and apparently not threatened.

Commerson's Dolphin
Cephalorhynchus commersonii
b: ≈0.75 m; sm: 1.28–1.3 m;
mx: ♀ 1.52 m, ♂ 1.49 m; 66–86 kg.
f: coastal bottom fish, crustaceans, and squid.
d: usually coastal waters around Kerguélen and Falkland Islands, and southeastern South America.
s: insufficiently known; may be threatened by illegal bait fisheries and incidental net entanglements.

Hector's Dolphin
Cephalorhynchus hectori
b: 0.6–0.7 m; sm: ♀ 1.35–1.39 m, ♂ 1.17–1.27 m; mx: ♀ 1.53 m, 57.3 kg; ♂ 1.38 m, 52.7 kg.
f: surface to benthic fish, squid.
d: coastal New Zealand waters off South Island, west of North Island.
s: indeterminate; limited range and net entanglements cause concern.

Heaviside's Dolphin
Cephalorhynchus heavisidii
b: 0.85 m; sm: 1.57–1.59 m;
mx: 1.74 m, 74.4 kg.
f: pelagic and inshore fish, cephalopods.
d: coastal southwest Africa from Namibia to Cape Town.
s: insufficiently known; direct and incidental takes cause concern.

Black (Chilean) Dolphin
Cephalorhynchus eutropia
b: <1 m; pm: ♀ >1.5 m, 33 kg; ♂ 1.52 m, 62 kg;
mx: ♀ 1.65 m, ♂ 1.67 m
f: cephalopods, fish, and shrimp.
d: coastal southwestern South America from about 30°S to the tip at 55°S.
s: insufficiently known; direct illegal take across its limited range raises a major concern.

Northern Right-whale Dolphin
Lissodelphis borealis
b: 0.8–1 m; sm: ♀≈2 m, ♂ 2.2 m;
mx: ♀ 2.3 m, ♂ 3.1 m; 115 kg.
f: squid and a variety of fish, especially lantern fish.
d: pelagic temperate North Pacific between about 50°N and 30°N.
s: insufficiently known; most common marine mammal caught incidentally in N. Pacific pelagic net fishery.

Southern Right-whale Dolphin
Lissodelphis peronii
b: 0.8–1 m; mx: ♀ 2.3 m, ♂ >2.1 m; 116 kg; few have been measured.
f: squid and a variety of fish, especially lantern fish.
d: circumpolar temperate to subantarctic Southern Hemisphere waters.
s: insufficiently known; may be taken incidentally by drift-net fisheries.

Short-beaked Common Dolphin
Delphinus delphis
b: 0.79–0.85 m; sm: ♀ 1.6 m, ♂ 1.7 m;
pm: ♀ 1.93 m, ♂ 2.01 m; ≈82 kg;
mx: ♀ 2 m, ♂ 2.19 m; ≈100 kg.
f: small pelagic fish and cephalopods.
d: all temperate and tropical waters of the world, also the Black Sea.
s: insufficiently known; common.

Long-beaked Common Dolphin
Delphinus capensis
b: 0.8–1.05 m; sm: ♀ 1.93 m, ♂ 2.02 m;
pm: ♀ 2.24 m, ♂ 2.42 m;
mx: ♀ 2.3 m, ♂ 2.6 m; 136 kg.
f: small pelagic fish and cephalopods
d: all temperate and tropical waters of the world.
s: insufficiently known; common.

Spinner Dolphin
Stenella longirostris
b: 0.7–0.8 m; sm: ♀ 1.65 m, ♂ 1.7 m;
pm: ♀ 2.1 m, ♂ 2.2 m; 80 kg;
mx: ♂ 2.38 m, five identified forms comprise three possible subspecies.
f: mesopelagic fish and squid.
d: pelagic subtropical through tropical zones worldwide.
s: insufficiently known; tens of thousands killed annually, directly and incidentally.

Clymene Dolphin
Stenella clymene
b: 0.75 m; sm: ♂ 1.76 m; pm: ♂ 1.97 m.
f: small mesopelagic fish and squid.
d: subtropical and tropical Atlantic Ocean and the Gulf of Mexico.
s: insufficiently known; possible incidental take by drift-net fisheries.

Pantropical Spotted Dolphin
Stenella attenuata
b: 0.85 m; sm: 1.6 m;
coastal form: ♀ 2.1 m, ♂ 2.23 m;
offshore form: ♀ 1.87 m; ♂ 2 m;
mx: ♀ 2.4 m, ♂ 2.6 m; >120 kg.
f: small epipelagic and mesopelagic fish and cephalopods.
d: pelagic tropical and, to a lesser extent, subtropical waters worldwide.
s: insufficiently known; major incidental takes by uncontrolled tuna fishery.

Atlantic Spotted Dolphin
Stenella frontalis
b: 0.88–1.2 m; avg: 2 m;
mx: ♀ 2.29 m, ♂ 2.26 m; 143 kg.
f: various cephalopods and fish.
d: tropical through subtropical and into the warm temperate Atlantic.
s: insufficiently known; suffers from purse-seine fishery for tuna in the eastern tropical Atlantic.

Striped Dolphin
Stenella coeruleoalba
b: ≈1 m; sm: 1.8–1.9 m; avg: ♀ 2.2 m, ♂ 2.3 m; mx: 2.6 m; 156 kg.
f: various mesopelagic fish, cephalopods, and crustaceans.
d: most pelagic warm temperate, subtropical, and tropical waters.
s: insufficiently known; often caught incidentally in pelagic net fishery.

Risso's Dolphin
Grampus griseus
b: 1.35–1.66 m; sm: ♀ 2.60–2.84 m, ♂ 2.62–2.97 m; mx: ♀ 3.66 m, ♂ 3.83 m; 500 kg.
f: cephalopods (especially squid), crustaceans, possibly some small fish.
d: pelagic tropical, subtropical, and temperate waters worldwide.
s: insufficiently known; taken in quantity by Sri Lanka gill-net fishery.

Irrawaddy Dolphin
Orcaella brevirostris
b: ≈0.85 m; sm: ≈2.1 m; ≈100 kg;
mx: ♀ 2.32 m, ♂ 2.75 m.
f: fish (especially carp), cephalopods, and crustaceans.
d: subtropical and tropical coastal to riverine waters of the Indo-Pacific.
s: insufficiently known; taken indirectly throughout its range.

Melon-headed Whale
Peponocephala electra
b: 0.65–1.12 m; sm: ♀ 2.29–2.57 m, ♂ 2.12–2.64 m;
mx: ♀ 2.75 m, ♂ 2.73 m; 275 kg.
f: squid and various small fish.
d: equatorial into subtropical waters.
s: insufficiently known; taken directly in small cetacean fisheries, incidentally by gill-net and seine fisheries.

Pygmy Killer Whale
Feresa attenuata
b: 0.53–0.82 m; sm: ♀ 2.2 m, ♂ 2 m;
mx: ♀ 2.43 m, ♂ 2.87 m; 225 kg.
f: small fish and squid.
d: all tropical and subtropical waters.
s: insufficiently known; no threats.

False Killer Whale
Pseudorca crassidens
b: ≈1.7 m; sm: ♀ 3.49–3.64 m, ♂ 3.7 m;
mx: ♀ 5.06 m, ♂ 5.96 m; 2,000 kg.
f: large fish, cephalopods, dolphins.
d: tropical, subtropical, and some temperate waters, worldwide.
s: insufficiently known; subject of conflicts with humans in fisheries.

Killer Whale
Orcinus orca
b: 1.83–2.74, 180 kg; sm: ♀ 4.6–5.4 m, ♂ 5.2–6.2 m; pm: ♀ 7 m, ♂ 8.2 m;
mx: ♀ 7.7 m; 7,500 kg, ♂ 9.0 m; 10,000 kg.
f: any vertebrate species they may encounter and desire, from fish to blue whales, gulls to moose.
d: all oceans, both hemispheres; from ice edge at high latitudes to the tropics.
s: insufficiently known; likely stable.

Short-finned Pilot Whale
Globicephala macrorhynchus
b: 1.4–1.8 m; pm: ♀ 5.25 m, ♂<6.1 m;
mx: ♀ 5.5 m, ♂ 6.75 m; <3,600 kg.
f: mainly various species of squid; occasionally, dolphins.
d: warm temperate, tropical waters.
s: insufficiently known; subject to deliberate and incidental takes.

Long-finned Pilot Whale
Globicephala melas [= *G. melaena*]
b: 1.77 m; sm: ♀ 3–4 m, ♂ 4–5 m;
mx: ♀ 5.70 m, ♂ 7.62 m; 2,000 kg.
f: various species of squid.
d: cold temperate to subantarctic oceans, including warm to cold temperate North Atlantic, middle to western Mediterranean Sea.
s: insufficiently known; extinct in Pacific, abundant in North Atlantic.

Narwhal
Monodon monoceros
b: 1.5–1.7 m; sm: ♀≈3.4 m, ♂ 3.9 m;
pm: ♀ 4 m, ♂ 4.7 m (without tusk);
mx: ♀ 5.1 m, ♂ 6.2 m; 1,600 kg.
f: cephalopods, fish (salmon, herring, cod, halibut, etc.), crustaceans.
d: above the Arctic Circle with a gap from eastern Russia to western Canada.
s: insufficiently known; indigenous peoples take in subsistence fishery.

Beluga (White Whale)
Delphinapterus leucas
b: 1.55 m, 80 kg; sm: ♀ 3 m, ♂ 3.6 m;
pm: ♀ 3.62 m; 900 kg, ♂ 4.27 m; 1,600 kg; mx: ♀<4.1 m, ♂<5.5 m.
f: Arctic cod, herring, smelt, flounder, various crustaceans, mollusks, and other benthic invertebrates.
d: Arctic and subarctic waters.
s: insufficiently known; some stocks have been reduced to 10–20% of original numbers by commercial whalers; pollution is a serious threat.

Harbor Porpoise
Phocoena phocoena
b: 0.7–0.9 m; pm: < 1.8 m; ≈ 45 kg;
mx: ♀ 1.89 m, ♂ 1.78 m; 70 kg.
f: benthic and pelagic fish, especially herring, mackerel, anchovy, and whiting; some benthic invertebrates.
d: shallow coastal waters, cool temperate to subarctic of N. Hemisphere.
s: insufficiently known; subject to major gill-net mortality and direct catch.

Burmeister's Porpoise
Phocoena spinipinnis
b: 0.85 m; pm: 1.8 m; mx: 2.0 m; 85 kg;
f: squid, small fish (hake, anchovy).
d: coastal South American waters, northern Peru to southern Brazil.
s: insufficiently known; suffers from incidental takes in gill nets.

Vaquita
Phocoena sinus
b: 0.70–0.75 m; pm: ♀ 1.5 m at 11 yrs, ♂ 1.4 m at 13–16 yrs; 36 kg;
mx: ♀ 1.5 m, ♂ 1.45 m; ≈50 kg.
d: squids, grunts, and gulf croakers
r: northernmost Sea of Cortez.
s: greatly endangered; at its genetic threshold; one population, small area.

Finless Porpoise
Neophocaena phocaenoides
b: ≈ 0.55–1.0 m; sm: ♀<1.41 m, ♂≈ 1.5 m; 36 kg; pm: < 1.6 m;
mx: ♀ 1.64 m, ♂ 1.87 m; 45 kg.
d: squid, prawn, cuttlefish, small fish.
r: warm riverine and coastal waters, Persian Gulf to Indonesia and Japan.
s: insufficiently known; extirpated in some places by habitat destruction.

Spectacled Porpoise
Australophocoena dioptrica
b: ≈0.5 m; sm: ♀<1.86 m at ≈50 kg;
mx: ♀ 2.04 m, ♂ 2.24 m; ≈84 kg.
d: squid and small fish.
r: near several Southern Hemisphere islands in cold temperate waters, also off southern South America.
s: insufficiently known; taken directly and incidentally by gill nets.

Dall's Porpoise
Phocoenoides dalli
b: 0.85–1.0 m; avg: 1.8 m; 125 kg;
mx: ♀ 2.2 m, ♂ 2.36 m; 220 kg.
d: squid, small fish such as hake, capelin, herring, and mackerel.
r: subarctic through warm temperate North Pacific; central Bering Sea to northern Baja California and Japan.
s: insufficiently known; in decline from heavy direct predation and incidental takes.

Key

Common Name
Taxonomic name (Genus species)
b: size at birth. **sm**: sexual maturity. **pm**: physical maturity. **avg**: average. **mx**: maximum known. **f**: food. **d**: distribution and habitat. **s**: status, designated by The World Conservation Union in *The IUCN Red Data Book*; "insufficiently known" is applied broadly. Length in meters, weight in kilos; (multiply by 3.3 to get feet, by 2.2 to get pounds).
Symbols: ♀ female, ♂ male; < less than, > greater than; ≈ approximate. Data is unavailable for all age/gender classes; figures apply to both sexes if no gender is given.

LIFE HISTORY DATA COMPILED, REVIEWED, AND EDITED BY PIETER AREND FOLKENS

Index

Boldface indicates illustrations.

Acoustic tracking 17, 111, 125, 128, 129, 224, 225
Aleuts: hunting of whales with poison darts 25, 27
Alling, Gay 56
Alvarez Colombo, Gustavo 43, **45**
Amazon River dolphins *see* Botos
Ambergris 62
American Society of Mammologists: appointment of international whaling commission 39
Amphipods 88; gray whale diet 98
Anchovy, southern: dolphin diet 142, 173, 177
Andrew's beaked whales **80**
Antarctica: blue whale population 86, slaughter of whales 38, numbers of blue and fin whales taken (1920-1971) 39; whale sanctuary 104
Archaeoceti (order) 22
Architeuthis 50
Arnoux's beaked whales **80**
Atlantic gray whales: extinction 31
Atlantic spotted dolphins **40, 138-139;**138-139; vocalizations 141
Atlantic white-sided dolphins 31, **164, 201**
Australia: whaling 33, **34-35,** prohibition of whaling 33
Azores (islands), Atlantic Ocean: whaling **32-33;** white sperm whale **51**

Bahamas: spotted dolphins **180-181, 182, 183,** 225
Baiji (Yangtze River dolphin) **185, 201;** endangered 184, **201,** 217, 222; rehabilitation efforts 187, 190
Baird's beaked whales 60, 72, **73, 80;** care of young by males 76
Baja California, Mexico: blue whales **96-97, 98;** bottlenose dolphins 164; gray whale calving grounds 21, 92, 121; whale-watchers petting gray whale **89**
Balaenidae (family) 93
Balaenopteridae (family) 93
baleeiro: aiming lance at wounded sperm whale 32, **33**
Baleen: definition 24-25, 92-93, 135; human uses 31
Baleen whales **82-137;** classification 93; evolution 24; number of species 93, 135; ocean migrations 125
Basques: whaling 31
Beaked whales 60, 61, **72-73,** 76; number of species 60, 182; skulls **58;** unidentified species **72**
Beale, Thomas: quoted on sperm whales 53
Béland, Pierre 187, **189**
Belugas **10-11,** 144, 145, **189, 191, 193, 201;** bloated dead whale **188;** captive **204,** 205; clicks 189; coordinated hunting 165; cow and calf **193;** curiosity 192; decline of St. Lawrence River population 187, 217; inbreeding 187; killed by polar bear **190;** melons 192; nickname 189, 217; population 189; satellite tracking **191,** 223; shedding of skin 27, **191;** skull 143; strandings **190;** toxic pollution 187, 189, 217; unfused neck vertebrae 143
Bhulans: endangered 184, 187, **201**
Bigg, Michael **158,** 212
Bioluminescence: sperm whales 76
Black dolphins **201;** commercial fishing 184
Blainville's beaked whales **72, 80;** skull **58**
Blue whales 93, 94, **98, 99, 136-137;** acoustic tracking 129, 224; baleen 97; cow and calf 86, **87;** feeding behavior 94, **96-97,** 103, 111, lunge feeding 103; feeding grounds 111; killer whale prey 168; lifespan 98; mating behavior 118; migrations 86, 112; photographic identification 86, 98, 103; populations 86, 103; protected status 184, 215; satellite tracking **100-101,** 111, 223; size 94, 118, 132; vocalizations 100, 128, 129; whaling 39, 184
Botos **184, 201;** captive 217, **218-219;** deaths 184; echolocation 217; predators 159; rescued **184,** 217; threats to 184
Bottlenose dolphins **4-5, 134, 140,** 142, **144,** 159, 165, 178-179, **201,** 206, **207, 209, 221;** captive **14-15,** returned to wild **220;** cooperation with fishermen 206; coordinated hunting 164; deaths 185-186; fission-fusion behavior 177-178; habitat degradation 185, 221; intelligence 152-153; mating behavior 184; size 144; solitary male 206; strandings **149;** studies of **144-145,** 177-179, 212, 221, 222; toxic accumulations 185, 217, 221; viral infections 185-186, 217
Bottlenose whales 60, 61, 69, 72, **74-75;** oil 69; spermaceti organ 72; studies of 72; ultrasonic clicks 72; whaling 69
Bowhead whales 93, **110, 112, 115, 136;** acoustic tracking 111, 125, 128, 224; baleen 110; endangered 116; feeding behavior 95, 105, 109; Inupiat hunters flensing **116-117;** migrations 112, 125; name origin 110; pectoral flipper 112, **113;** population 111, prewhaling population 111; satellite tracking 110-111, 223; whaling 31, 116, 184
British Columbia: whale fossils 22
Brower, Eugene **116**
Brower, Frederick 116, **117**
Brown, Miranda 113
Brown, Moira 119
Bryde's whales 93, 94, **136;** breaching **108,** 109; habitat 109; prey 109
Burmeister's porpoises **200**

Calambokidis, John 103
Capelin: humpback whale diet 109
Carlson, Carole 92, 121
Cascadia Research Collective 103
Center for Coastal Studies 105, 113, 121
Center for Whale Studies 121
Cetacea (order) 153
Chile: ban on dolphin harvesting 187
Clapham, Phil 113
Clark, Christopher W. 92, 111, 125, 129, 224
Clymene dolphins **201**
Commerson's dolphins **201;** commercial fishing 184
Common dolphins 143, **169,** 190, **201**
Connor, Richard 178, 179
Copepods 97, 105, 109
Costa Rica: sperm whales **76-77;** spotted dolphins **198-199**
Crozet Islands, Indian Ocean: killer whales 168
Curtsinger, Bill 126, 212, 214
Cuvier's beaked whales 60, **80**

Dall's porpoises **200;** harvesting of **176**
Darling, James D. **45,** 85, 212, 214, 232
Dawson, Steve **62,** 187
Delphinidae (family) 142
Denjiro, Hosono **40**
Devilfish (gray whales) 33
Diatoms **97**
Die-offs 185-186, 187, **188,** 189, 217
Dingle Bay, Ireland: bottlenose dolphin and terrier 206, **207**
Discovery Committee: whale research 39-40, 222
DNA research 58, 223, 224
Dolphins **138-199;** blowholes 145, 150; captive **146, 147;** clicks 142, 149-150; cooperative fish hunts with people 190, 206; coordinated hunting 164; differences from porpoises 142, 153; echolocation 150, 152, 164, 196; fishing net deaths **168;** fission-fusion behavior 173; intelligence 41, 152-153, 192; mating behavior 196; melons 152, 196; monkey lips 150; multispecies aggregations 159; number of species 142, 153; predators 145; revered by ancient Greeks and Romans 190, 206; senses: hearing 149, "jaw hearing" 152, smell 145, tactile 148-149, taste 145, 148, visual acuity 149; skull 143; slaughter **170-171;** sleep physiology 149, 196; sociality 153; teeth 142, 153; testes 179; toxic accumulations 186; ungulate ancestry 143-144, 150; *see also* Killer whales; *and* species *by name*
Dorsey, Ellie 214
Dorudontinae (order) 22
Dosidicus gigas 50
Drift nets: destruction of marine life 187, 216; United Nations ban (1992) 187, 216, 217
Dusky dolphins 141-142, 144, **164,** 190, **201, 223;** commercial fishing 184; coordinated hunting 168-169, 173; diving ability 164; echolocation 142, clicks 142, 164, 169; feeding 176-177; fission-fusion behavior 173, 176-177; killer whale prey 153; mating behavior 173; migrations 177; prey 142, 169, 177; studies of 223
Dutch (people): whaling 22
Dwarf sperm whales 60, 76, **81**

Ellis, Graeme 206, 214
Eschrichtiidae (family) 93
Eskimos, Polar: narwhal hunting **172, 173**
European Union: whaling ban 32

False killer whales **150,** 159, **200;** echolocating clicks 150; strandings **149**
Faroe Islands, North Atlantic Ocean: whaling **30**
Faucher, Annick 72
Ferrari, Mark 214
Fin whales 93, 94, **136-137;** asymmetrical coloration **84,** 85, 93-94; caught in gill net 212; feeding behavior 94, 105, echelon feeding 105, **106-107;** protected status 184; vocalizations 128; whaling 39, 184
Finless porpoises **179, 200;** fishing net deaths 184
Finley, Kerry 105, 109, 112, **113, 114**
Foott, Jeff 156
Ford, John K. B. **165,** 206, 214
Fordyce, R. Ewan 23
Foyn, Svend 38
France: use of large-scale drift nets 187
Franciscana (La Plata dolphins) **201**
Fristrup, Kurt 51
Fundy, Bay of, Canada: release of harbor porpoise **177**
Futo, Japan: slaughter of striped dolphins **170-171**

Gagnon, Chuck 129
Galápagos Islands, Pacific Ocean: sperm whales **46-47,** 56-59, **60, 61, 66-67**
Garciarena, David **126**
Gervais' beaked whales **81**
Giddings, Al 214
Gill nets: destruction of marine life **186,** 187, 212
Gilligan, Philip **64-65**
Gingerich, Philip 22
Ginkgo-toothed beaked whales 60, **80**
Glockner-Ferrari, Deborah A. 121, 214
Gordon, Jonathan 49, 57, 58, **60**
Gray whales **12-13,** 25, **89,** 93, **136;** attacks on humans 21-22, 33, 38; baleen **88;** barnacle-encrusted skin **88, 89;** breaching 92, **93;** breeding and calving grounds 92, 121; calves 121; extinction of Atlantic gray 31; feeding behavior 89, **90-91,** 95, 98, 105, bottom feeding **94,** 95, **95,** 98, 105; feeding grounds 92; gestation 119; lithograph of **27;** migrations 92, 98, 111-112; Okhotsk-Korean population 95, 98; protected status 184, 215; rescue of **210-211;** reproduction 121; skin parasites **88,** 92; spy hopping **88;** studies of 92, 98, 212; tracking 22; vocalizations 128; whaling 25, 184
Gray's beaked whales **81**
Greenpeace activists: **214,** 215
Griffin, Edward I. "Ted" 36; swimming with killer whale **39**
grindadráp (whale killing) 31
Gully (submarine canyon), North Atlantic Ocean 61, 69, 72, 73

Harbor porpoises 143, 144, 145, **200;** intelligence 152; released from herring trap **177**
Hartenberger, Jean-Louis 22
Heaviside's dolphins **201**
Hector's beaked whales **81**
Hector's dolphins 142, 145, 190 **201;** drowned in gill net **186,** 187; habitat 159; sanctuary 187
Herzing, Denise **180-181,** 225
Honshū (island), Japan: harvesting of Dall's porpoises **176**
Hooker, Sascha **66**
Hourglass dolphins **164, 201**
Hubbs' beaked whales **80**
Hump-backed dolphins **179, 201;** habitat degradation 185
Humpback whales **1,** 17, 86-87, 93, 109, 125, **137, 201, 231;** acoustic tracking 224; baleen 132, **133;** breaching **1,** 119, **120;** breeding and calving grounds 92, 121; cow and calf 121, **122-123, 124,** 125, **134-135,** 225, **226-227,** die-off 217; feeding behavior 105, 109, **132-133,** bubblenet feeding 95, 98, 102-103; feeding grounds 110; genus 93; mating behavior 87, 89, 113, 118, 121, **122-123, 124, 125,** 214; migrations 89, 92, 112-113, 121; pectoral flippers 119, **120;** protected status 184, 215; reproduction 121, gestation 119; satellite tracking 110, 223; scientific name 119; song 85-86, 89, 92, 102, 113, 118, singing 86, 113, **125**

Indian Ocean Whale Sanctuary 49
Indonesia: dolphin tourism 191
Indus River dolphins 217; *see also* Bhulans
Integrated Undersea Surveillance System 17, 129, 224
International Convention for the Regulation of Whaling 38-39
International Union for the Conservation of Nature and Natural Resources (IUCN) 187
International Whaling Commission (IWC) 38-39, 116; establishment of Antarctic whale sanctuary (1994) 104; moratorium on commercial whaling (1986), 103, 104, 215
International Wildlife Coalition 93
Inuit 217; hunting of belugas 27, 30
Inupiat: boys studying **211;** rescue of gray whales **210-211;** whaling **116-117,** 211, 215
Irrawaddy dolphins 144-145, 191, **201;** habitat degradation 185
Isabella Bay, Baffin Island: whale sanctuary 112
Italy: use of large-scale drift nets 187

Jan Mayen (island), Norway: whaling 31
Japan: ban on large-scale drift nets 187; harvesting of Dall's porpoises **176;** pro-whaling agenda 105, 215; research 215; whale-watching 109, 191; whalers' parade **40;** whaling **25,** 104, **105,** 215
Jones, Mary Lou 92, 212
Jurasz, Charles (Chuck) 89, 95, 98, 102
Jurasz, Virginia 89

Kaikoura, New Zealand: dusky dolphins **223;** sperm whale **62;** whale-watching 190-191, **222,** 223
Kasuya, Toshio 60
Katona, Steven K. 92, 212, 217
Kerr, Iain **224**
Killer whales **39,** 142, 144, 158, **159-163, 200, 202-203,** 212; attacking seal pups **156-157;** attacks on sperm whales 57-58; breaching **197;** captive 36, **37, 39, 160-161,** first captive-born, 160, **162-163,** injuries to trainers 160, limitation of gene pool 160, public protests against captivity **36;** coordinated hunting 165, 168; dorsal fins 142, **158,** 182; family groups 158; misconceptions about 38; patrolling surf **156;** pods 165, 182; prey 38, 145, 153, 156, **157,** 165, 168, 217; rubbing beach **159,** 205, 206, 225; scientific name 38; sexual dimorphism 182; strandings **149;** *see also* Namu
Kittigaruit, Northwest Territories, Canada: beluga whale hunting 27, 30
Komori, Shigeki 109
Korea, South: ban on large-scale drift nets 187
Kraus, Scott D. 92, 111, 118, 119
Krill **97;** baleen whale diet 97, 102, 103, 119

LaBudde, Samuel **168**
Leatherwood, Stephen 187
Lembata Island, Indonesia: sperm whale hunting **212, 213**
Lii (bottlenose dolphin) **144**
Longman's beaked whales 60, **81**

Makah: whale hunting 24, 25
Marine Mammal Protection Act (1972) 168
Marineland of Florida: performing dolphin, **40**
Martineau, Daniel 187
Mate, Bruce **100, 101,** 110, 111
Mayo, Charles "Stormy" 92, 105, 109
McVay, Scott 85
Mead, James **58**
Mediterranean Sea: striped dolphin die-off 185, 217
Melon-headed whales **200**
Melville, Herman 50; quoted on sperm whales 53, 67
Mercury 31; poisoning of dolphins 221
Mesoplodon species A **81**
Mexico, Gulf of: bottlenose dolphin die-off 186, 217
Milinkovitch, Michel 60
Miller, Karen 86
Mingan Island Cetacean Study 98, 103
Minke whales **26,** 27, **82-83,** 85, 93, 94, **136-137;** feeding behavior 94, 95, 105, lunge feeding **102,** 103; fetus **215;** prey 95, 105; whaling **103, 104, 105,** 215
Moby Dick (Melville) 24, 53, 225
Møhl, Bertel 56
Monkey Mia, Western Australia, Australia: bottlenose dolphins 178-179
Monodontidae (family) 143
Muktuk 30, 116, **173,** 192
Mysticeti (suborder) 24, 92

Nakamura, Koji 98
Namu (killer whale) **37, 39;** death in captivity 36
Nantucket (island), Mass.: whaling 33
Narwhals **174-175, 201;** bulls **16, 172,** 182; butchering site **173;** coordinated hunting 165; nickname 172; sexual dimorphism 182; skull 143; tusks **16,** 17, bulls sparring with, **172,** 182; unfused neck vertebrae 143
National Geographic Society: support of cetacean research 17, 27, 43
Neobalaenidae (family) 93

230 WHALES

GRACEFUL HUMPBACK Silhouetted just below the surface, a humpback seems to hover in the cold, greenish waters off Newfoundland.

BILL CURTSINGER

New Bedford, Mass.: whaling 33
New Zealand: dolphin sanctuary 187; dolphins 153, 159, 177, 190; fishing net size regulations 187; killer whales 153; sperm whales **53**, 62; whale-watching 190, 191, **222**, 223
Nicklin, Charles "Flip" 50, 69, 86, 112, **126**, 183, 192, 205, 232
Nicklin, Chuck 86, 207, 212
Nicklin, Gloria 212
Nicklin, Terry 62, **64-65**, 212
Nootka: whaling 25
Norris, Kenneth S. 21, 41, **56**, 152, 159, 177, 232
Northern bottlenose whales 60, 61, 69, 73, **74-75, 81**
Northern right-whale dolphins **178, 200**
Northern right whales 93, **136**; DNA studies 119, 121; endangered status 119; migration 112; reproduction 119, 121; whaling 184
Norway: minke whaling **103, 214**, 215

Odontocetes (family) 50, 53, 135
Odontoceti (suborder) 24
Okhotsk, Sea of: gray whale population 95, 98; whaling 33
Olympic Peninsula, Washington: Makah 25; whale petroglyph **24**
Orcas *see* Killer whales
Oregon: beached sperm whales 67
Östman-Lind, Jan **166**

Ozette (site), Washington 24, 25
Pacific white-sided dolphins **165, 201**
Pakicetus inachus 22
Pakistan: discovery of ancient whale skull 22
Patenaude, Nathalie 187
Payne, Katy 85, 86, 89, 92, 111, 168
Payne, Roger **45**, 85, 86, 89, 92, 111, 129, 168, 212, 222, 223; monitoring whale vocalizations **42-43**
Payne, Sam **111**
PCB contamination: belugas 187; dolphins 221; sperm whales 73
Peale's dolphins **201**
Perrin, William 187
Peru: ban on dolphin harvesting 187
Philippines: ban on dolphin harvesting 187
Pilot whales **142, 151**, 164, **200**; coordinated hunting 165; diving ability 145; echolocation, clicks 164; killed by whalers in shallows **30**, 31, 142; melons 150; nursing calves 142, **143**, 182; pods 142; scars 150; sexual dimorphism 182; strandings 142
Plutarch: quoted on dolphins 206
Point Barrow, Alaska: monitoring of bowhead whale vocalizations **111**
Porpoises: differences from dolphins 142, 153; echolocation 196; melons 196; number of species 142, 153; sleep physiology 196; teeth 142, 153;

see also individual species
Pruna, Andy **43**
Pryor, Karen 41
Purse-seine tuna fishing: dolphin deaths 166
Pygmy beaked whales 58, 60, **80**; skull 58
Pygmy killer whales **150, 200**
Pygmy right whales 93, **136**
Pygmy sperm whales 60, 76, **81**

Qaqqasiq, Apak 112

Ray, John 152
Read, Andrew **177**
Reeves, Randall 187
Richard, Kenny 58
Right-whale dolphins: absence of dorsal fin 142
Right whales 109; calves 125, laying fluke across mother's blowhole **129**; endangered 119; feeding behavior 105; flukes **44-45, 129, 130-131**; gestation 119; mating behavior 118-119; prey 105; protected status 184, 215; satellite tracking 111; studies of 43, 92, 111, 121, 212, 222; whaling 22, 33, 184; *see also* Northern right whales; Pygmy right whales; Southern right whales
Risso's dolphins **152**, 164, **200**
River dolphins 142, 143, **184, 217**, **218-219**; intelligence 152; threats to 217, 222
Robertson, R. B. 40
Rorquals 38, 93, 94, 103, 109
Rosenthal, Rick **77**
Rough-toothed dolphins 41, 152-153, **154-155, 201**

Sanctuaries 49, 104, 112, 187
Satellite tracking **100-101**, 110-111, 223-224
Sayigh, Laela 149
Scammon, Charles M. 21; lithograph by **27**; quoted on whales and whaling 33, 111
Schaeff, Catherine 119
Schulke, Flip 38, 214
Scoresby, William: quoted on whales 31
Sea Life Park, Oahu, Hawaii: rough-toothed dolphins 41
Sea lions **156**; pups 156, **157**
Sea World, San Diego, California: killer whales **160-161**
Sears, Richard 86, **98**, 103, 118
Sei whales 93, 94, **118**, 119, **136-137**; protected status 184; whaling 119, 184
Seymour Peninsula, Antarctica: whale fossils 22
Shepherd's beaked whales 60, **81**
Shrimp, ghost: gray whale diet 98
Silber, Greg 87, 214
Similä, Tiu 168
Slooten, Elisabeth 187
Smolker, Rachel 178, 179
Smultea, Mari **225**
Southern bottlenose whales **80**
Southern dusky dolphins: pods 179
Southern right-whale dolphins **178, 200**
Southern right whales **2-3, 43**, 93, 121, **126-127, 128, 137**, 168; breeding and calving grounds 121, 125, 126; cows and calves **6-7**, 121, 125, **126, 127**; flukes **44-45, 126, 129, 130-131**; studies of 43, 121, 125, 168
Sowerby's beaked whales **81**
Spectacled porpoises **200**
Sperm whales 17, **46-48**, 50, **51-53, 56-57, 61, 66-69, 76-79, 81**, 190; births 57; brain size 50, 58; calves **51, 61, 70-71**, care of 57, 68; carcasses **28-29**; caught in net 216, deaths 73, freed from **64-65**; clicks 72, 76, codas 56-57, 60, echocodas 76; courtship behavior 59; diving 52, 56, **57, 63, 68, 222**; feces 50, squid beaks found in 62; feeding behavior 51, 53, 56; flukes **54-55, 63**; habitat 50; migrations 62; museu de singe 50-51; nickname 51; oxygen storage 56, 69; PCB contamination 73; painting of **20**; satellite tracking 223; scientific name 50; sexual dimorphism 182; size 50, 53; skeleton, juvenile **8-9, 59**; social behavior 56, 58, 59, **68, 69**, 76; spermaceti organ 50-51, 53; strandings 67, 212; studies of 50, 51, 57, 67, 224, **225**, DNA studies 58; teeth 53, 67; tracking 56, **60**, 62; whaling 33, **34-35**, 49, 53, 59, 68, **212, 213**, flensing 32, harpooned 20, 32, **33**, 212, 213; white sperm whales 50, **51**
Spinner dolphins 144, 159, **166-167, 201**; clicks 153, 159; feeding 177; fishing net deaths 166; fission-fusion behavior 177; pods 179; predators 159; prey 159, 166; sexual dimorphism 182; studies of 41; teeth 166; videotaped underwater **166-67**
Spitsbergen (island), Norway: whaling 31
Spotted dolphins **138-139**, 143, 144, 159, **180-183, 198-199, 201**; coordinated hunting 164-165, **182**, 183; juvenile coloration 183; mating **182**, 183; performing at oceanarium **40**; studies of **180-181**, 183, 225
Squid: whale diet 50, 73, 223
Stejneger's beaked whales 58, **80**; skull 58
Strap-toothed whales 58, 60, **80**; skull 58
Striped dolphins 144, **201**; die-off 186, 217; slaughtered **170-171**; viral infections 185-186
Suarez, José 38
Susu (Ganges River dolphins) **201**
Swartz, Steven L. 92, 212

Taber, Sara 121
Tadoussac, Quebec, Canada: necropsy of belugas 189
Taiji, Japan: whalers' parade **40**
Tethys Sea (ancient sea) 22
Thomas, Peter 92, 121
True's beaked whales 60, **81**
Tucuxi 144-45, **184, 201**, 217; captive **217**
Tuna fishing: ban on purse-seine nets 168; dolphin fatalities 168
Tyack, Peter 214

Vaquita 177; endangered status 184, 187; fishing net deaths **177**
Video probe: sperm whale research **224**

Watkins, William 59
Weilgart, Lindy 56, 57, 59, 76, 232
Wells, Randall 177, 212, 222
Whale Conservation Institute 224
Whale lice **88, 89**, 128
Whale-watching 109, **222**, 223, 225, 232
Whales: ancient skull 22; barometer of oceans' health 217; bones **18-19**; evolution 22-25; Latin name 61; ocean migrations 112-113; petroglyph **24**; products from 31; toxic accumulations 31; ungulate ancestry 143-144, 150; *see also* individual species
Whaling: history of **20**, 22, **23**, 24, **25**, **25**, 27, **27**, 30-33, 38-40, 215
White-beaked dolphins **201**
White-sided dolphins 31; *see also* Atlantic or Pacific white-sided dolphins
White whales *see* Belugas
Whitehead, Hal 49, 67, 92, 109, 223, 232; tracking sperm whales **60, 61**
Whitehead, Stefanie **60**, 225
Wild Dolphin Project 179, 225
Wiley, Dave 93-94
World Wide Fund for Nature/Japan 109
Wuhan Institute of Hydrobiology 190
Würsig, Bernd 95, 141, **223**, 232
Würsig, Melany 168, 190

Yangtze River dolphins *see* Baiji

Zhou Kaiya 190

Library of Congress CIP data

Whales, dolphins, and porpoises / prepared by the Book Division, National Geographic Society, Washington ; [contributing authors, Kenneth S. Norris ... et al.].
  p. cm.
Includes index.
ISBN 0-7922-2952-5 (reg.). — ISBN 0-7922-2953-3 (deluxe)
1. Whales. 2. Dolphins. 3. Porpoises. 4. Whales—Pictorial works. 5. Dolphins—Pictorial works. 6. Porpoises—Pictorial works. I. Norris, Kenneth S. (Kenneth Stafford) II. National Geographic Society (U.S.). Book Division.
QL737.C4W4425 1995
599.5—dc20   95-20916
                                                                                                                      CIP

INDEX

Authors' Statement

Our goal for this book is twofold: First, to update what we know about cetaceans, based on the last two decades of scientific research; second, to underscore the fact that cetaceans depend upon a healthy biosphere. Our desire is to see humans, as major players in determining the health of the biosphere, work toward bringing it into balance.

This desire does not stem merely from wanting to save whales. Rather, our motivation is logically based on a broader understanding: The system won't work for very much longer—for whales or for people—if present trends toward a degraded environment continue. We have a choice: Either we allow the human population to keep on expanding and to keep using natural resources beyond the earth's capacity to bear and renew, or we acknowledge the limits of the system and show restraint as individuals and as a species.

We hope that this book increases your understanding of, and admiration for, all the diverse cetaceans. We also hope that it dramatizes the urgent need for moderation on the part of the diverse human family. If so, then the whales will have spoken to you, through these words and photographs, even as they speak to us, whenever we meet them in their own domain.

About the Authors

JAMES D. DARLING, director of the West Coast Whale Research Foundation, was one of the first scientists to develop photographic techniques to identify individual whales as a basis for long-term study. Darling is recognized internationally for his work on gray whale and humpback whale behavior. His deep fascination with the social organization and ecology of baleen whales guides much of his current work. Darling initiated the first study of living baleen whales in Japan and is credited with a significant role in developing the now booming whale-watching industry in that country.

CHARLES "FLIP" NICKLIN began his underwater adventures swimming with his father, diving pioneer and underwater cinematographer Chuck Nicklin. By 1979 Flip Nicklin was photographing humpback whales for NATIONAL GEOGRAPHIC magazine. Since then, his work has been featured in 11 GEOGRAPHIC articles, as well as in numerous other publications. As creative consultant for the volume you hold in your hands, Nicklin has been instrumental in molding it into a medium to advance our appreciation of whales.

KENNETH S. NORRIS, professor of natural history at the University of California, Santa Cruz, is one of America's senior marine mammalogists. He has spent 40 years as a leader of pioneering cetacean studies and as a teacher and role model for successive waves of graduate students. Norris was one of the first to tell the story of dolphin echolocation. He discovered how dolphins propagate beams of sound through their foreheads and receive them through the sides of their jaws and tongues. Norris was among those who founded the Society for Marine Mammalogy, the major international scientific society for the study of marine mammals, and was its first president.

HAL WHITEHEAD, associate professor of biology at Dalhousie University in Halifax, Nova Scotia, has spent much of the past 20 years at sea on sailing boats studying the lives of whales, especially the whales of deep waters. Often accompanying him are his wife, Dr. Linda Weilgart, who studies the sounds of the whales, and their children, Benjamin, Stefanie, and Sonja. A trained statistician, Whitehead has developed statistical techniques to extract the most knowledge possible from the behavioral, photographic, acoustic, genetic, and ecological data collected during research voyages.

BERND WÜRSIG, professor of marine biology at Texas A&M University and director of the Marine Mammal Research Program there, has studied habitat use patterns and social behavior of whales and dolphins since 1972. After beginning his career studying dolphins, Würsig spent 14 years concentrating on the foraging and social behavior of bowhead whales in the Beaufort Sea of Canada and Alaska. Only in the past six years has he returned to his first love—social strategies of delphinids, currently focusing on these animals in the Gulf of Mexico and off New Zealand.

Whale-Watching Sites in North America and Hawaii

The sites listed below are among those known to be visited seasonally by certain species of whales. When you go whale-watching, keep your eyes open for other species in the area as well. For more information, consult *Where the Whales Are* by Patricia Corrigan. Guidelines for whale-watching are available by writing to the National Marine Fisheries Service, Office of Protected Resources, 1335 East-West Highway, Silver Spring, MD 20910.

NORTHEAST U.S.: HUMPBACKS—summer, numerous towns in Maine, Massachusetts, New Hampshire. Humpbacks are the main attraction; you also may see finback whales, minkes, occasionally the rare northern right whale, and assorted dolphins.
PACIFIC NORTHWEST: KILLER WHALES AND MINKES—summer, San Juan Islands, Washington; GRAY WHALES—March through May, Westport, Washington; December and January and March through May, Depoe Bay, Oregon.
CALIFORNIA: GRAY WHALES—late December through April, most coastal towns and cities, such as Point Arena, San Francisco, Half Moon Bay, Monterey, Santa Barbara, Ventura, San Diego; BLUE WHALES—summer, Santa Barbara, the Farallon Islands.
HAWAII: HUMPBACKS—January through March, Maui (Lahaina).
ALASKA: HUMPBACKS AND KILLER WHALES—summer, southeast Alaska (Glacier Bay, Gustavus, Admiralty Island, Sitka) and Prince William Sound.
WESTERN CANADA: GRAY WHALES—spring and summer; KILLER WHALES—summer, British Columbia (Vancouver Island and Queen Charlotte Islands).
EASTERN CANADA: BLUE WHALES, FINBACK WHALES, AND BELUGAS—summer, St. Lawrence River, Quebec; BELUGAS—summer, Manitoba (Churchill River and Hudson Bay) and Northwest Territories (Somerset Island); NARWHALS—summer, Northwest Territories (Baffin Island).
MEXICO: GRAY WHALES—January through March (peak February), Baja California (Scammon Lagoon, San Ignacio Lagoon, Magdalena Bay). Most tours depart from San Diego, California.

Additional Reading

The reader may wish to consult the *National Geographic Index* for related articles and books. The following titles may also be of interest: Roger Payne, *Among Whales;* Gaetano Cafiero and Maddalena Jahoda, *Giants of the Sea;* Erich Hoyt, *Meeting the Whales;* Kenneth S. Norris, *Dolphin Days;* R. B. Robertson, *Of Whales and Men;* Kenneth Brower and William R. Curtsinger, *Wake of the Whale;* Facts on File, *WHALES Dolphins and Porpoises;* James Darling and Flip Nicklin, *With the Whales;* Richard C. Connor and Dawn Micklethwaite Peterson, *The Lives of Whales and Dolphins;* Charles M. Scammon, *The Marine Mammals of the North-western Coast of North America;* Scott Kraus and Kenneth Mallory, *The Search for the Right Whale;* Stephen Leatherwood and Randall R. Reeves, *Sierra Club Handbook of Whales and Dolphins.*

Acknowledgments

The Book Division wishes to thank the individuals, groups, and organizations named or quoted in the text. In addition, we are grateful for the assistance of Lisa Atkinson; Lawrence G. Barnes; Kimberly Blankenbeker; Kevin Chu; Dot Delaney; David D'King; Connie Gordon; Katherine A. Hanly; Gordon L. Kirkland, Jr.; Donald Kyte; Glenn Moffat; Clyde Roper; Jan Timbrook; Craig Van Note; Joanne Whaley; and Graham Worthy.

Note: Photographs by Mark J. Ferrari and Deborah A. Glockner-Ferrari were taken under a scientific permit granted by the National Marine Fisheries Service and a scientific collecting permit granted by the State of Hawaii, Department of Land and Natural Resources.

Composition for this book by the National Geographic Society Book Division, with the assistance of the Typographic Section of National Geographic Production Services, Pre-Press Division. Printed and bound by R. R. Donnelley & Sons, Willard, Ohio. Color separations by Digital Color Image, Cherry Hill, N.J.; Graphic Art Services, Inc., Nashville, Tenn.; Lanman Progressive Co., Washington, D.C.; North American Color, Inc., Portage, Mich. Paper by Consolidated / Alling & Cory, Willow Grove, Penn. Dust jacket printed by Inland Press, Menomonee Falls, Wisc.